David W. Bercot

LET ME DIE IN IRELAND

The True Story of Patrick

SCROLL
PUBLISHING

Published by Scroll Publishing Company, P. O. Box 122, Amberson, PA 17210. (717) 349-7033.

ISBN: 092-4722-088

Cover photograph © David Bercot.

Printed in the United States of America

For a free catalog of other works published by Scroll Publishing Co., simply write or phone us at the address and telephone number above.

Our website: www.scrollpublishing.com.

Table of Contents

Forward

Practically everyone in the western world has heard of the man called St. Patrick. However, hardly anyone knows anything about him. About the only two things that most people "know" about Patrick is that he was Irish and Roman Catholic. In truth, he was neither. He was British, and he belonged to the independent Celtic Church. Although Patrick is the most famous person of his age, the real man has been buried under a cloud of myths. Myths such as:

- He used the shamrock to explain the Trinity.
- He was sent to Ireland by the Pope.
- He was a wonder-worker who staged miraculous duels with the Druids.
- He drove all of the snakes out of Ireland.

Even the famous hymn known as the "Lorica" or "Breast-Plate of St. Patrick" (which is one of my favorite hymns) was not written by Patrick. It doesn't even reflect Patrick's thoughts and spirituality.

Sadly, it's our loss that the real Patrick has been hidden in this cloud of fables. Christians today can learn much from the life of the real Patrick. In particular, his life reveals how God can do exceptional things with ordinary people. It also teaches us the need to persevere in prayer and to wait on God. The real Patrick was a fairly ordinary Christian, with an extraordinary prayer life. Prayer and faith were the keys to his success—not staging dramatic miracles. At the same time, God *did* intervene miraculously in Patrick's life, just as He intervenes in the lives of praying Christians today. In contrast, there is very little we can learn from the mythical Patrick–other than that if we could perform incredible miracles perhaps we, too, could convert a nation.

Ironically, the life of the real Patrick is just as fascinating as that of his mythical counterpart, if not more so. There's certainly no need to embellish his life with a lot of fables. He gave up a comfortable life as an upper-class citizen of Roman Britain to live in poverty, suffering, and constant danger in Ireland. Forsaking all, he brought Christ's love to the hated enemies of his own people—to the very nation who had once kidnapped and enslaved him. Although ridiculed and rejected by his own people in Britain, Patrick changed the course of an entire nation. He was one of the greatest missionaries who ever lived.

Why the Mythical Patrick Was Created

Sadly, outside of Ireland, Patrick was hardly known in his own lifetime (c. 385-461). By the time most of the European church had heard about Patrick, Western civilization had collapsed and the Middle Ages had set in. By then, few persons had any concept of history as a science. Medieval writers of history were not as concerned about the authenticity of their information as they were in telling a good story. It's usually difficult to sort fact from fable in the histories written during the Middle Ages.

Furthermore, by medieval times, most professing Christians had lost any understanding of the force of the Gospel when powerfully preached by a godly man of integrity. After A. D. 600, Western "Christianity" spread primarily through the influence of kings and the power of the sword—although there were some exceptions. So the medieval chroniclers had no grasp of how a simple man of prayer and faith could have had such an impact on a whole nation. In their minds, Patrick's success must have been attributable to dramatic miracles. In reality, what converted Patrick's hearers were not sensational miracles—but the power of the Gospel and the convicting force of the Holy Spirit. Not only were Patrick's words powerful, but his whole life was an incredible witness to the potency of love, faith, and prayer.

How I Have Re-Told the Story
of the Real Patrick

Our only genuine sources of historical information about Patrick are the two brief writings he has left us: his *Testimony*[1] and his letter of excommunication sent to the British king, Coroticus. Accordingly, in writing this biography, I first prepared a list of all the events he mentions in his two works, putting the events in their probable chronological order. That gave me the blueprint for the present work. At the end of each chapter, I have noted from which chapters of Patrick's *Testimony* (*Confessio*) or letter of excommunication (*Epistolo*) my information has come.

Unfortunately, Patrick's writings provide us with only a bare outline of the events of his life. To be sure, they do tell us a lot about Patrick: his personality, his thoughts, his spirituality, and his emotions. But they furnish us with precious few details about anything else. They give us only brief allusions to what was happening in the Roman world around him. They say virtually nothing about daily life in fifth-century Ireland and Britain. And they provide only sketchy descriptions of other persons who interacted with Patrick.

So, to tell the true story of Patrick—one that realistically describes the world he lived in—I have had to re-construct from other sources the historical background and the details of everyday life in Patrick's day. I have primarily used Bede's *Ecclesiastical History* to furnish the historical details about the collapse of Roman Britain and the coming of the Angles and Saxons. For my details about daily life, I have drawn from both ancient Roman writers and modern historical works. I have used the works of the Nicene and pre-Nicene Christian writers for my details on church life and methods of evangelism in Patrick's day. To familiarize myself with the land and climate of Ireland and Britain, I spent several weeks in those places during different seasons–walking on the same soil that Patrick trod, experiencing the same weather he did, gazing at the identical hills and rocky beaches that he looked at.

Equipped with this supplemental information, I have taken each event that Patrick mentions in his writings and tried to put myself at the scene of action, asking myself questions such as: How did this scene look? What were the houses like? How were the people dressed? What would have been the topics of conversation? How did the landscape

---

[1]*Confessio*, the Latin name of this work, is usually translated as *Confession*. However, *Testimony* more accurately renders the meaning of *Confessio* in Patrick's day.

look? What was the weather like? Without these historical details, we have only an extended encyclopedic treatise on Patrick—not his life story. In Appendix Two, I have set forth some of my suppositions and other notes concerning this supplemental information.

As you will discover, I have used dialogue to relate most of the events of Patrick's life. Obviously, in reconstructing such dialogue, I've exercised a bit of artistic license. However, when it is God who is speaking to Patrick in one of his dreams, I have used Patrick's literal language and footnoted where the passage can be found.

Reconstructing the people who surrounded Patrick has been the hardest challenge. Although Patrick mentions numerous people, he furnishes us with only four actual names: his grandfather, Potitus; his father, Calpornius; a man named Victoricus, who appears in a dream; and the petty British king, Coroticus. To bring Patrick's story to life, I have had to look elsewhere for the names and personalities of the people with whom he interacted. When possible, I have used names provided by Patrick's seventh century biographers, Muirchu and Tirechan. Otherwise, I've simply assigned typical period names to the people of Patrick's life. In Appendix Two, I have listed the names of the major people appearing in this biography and have explained whether they are historical, traditional, or literary.

Acknowledgments

Special thanks go to my wonderful wife Deborah, who encouraged me on this book and tirelessly proofread my manuscript. Thanks to our children—Andre, Heather, and Isaiah—who have never tired of hearing me relate the story of Patrick's life. I am most grateful to Mike Wood, Jim Freeman, Chester Weaver, and Stephen Jayne for their helpful input. I cannot thank Alex Alexander enough for his skillful help in designing the cover. I give my thanks to the kind people of Ireland who helped me get to know both the people and land of that beautiful country. Most of all, I am deeply indebted to Jeleta Eckheart, my editor, without whose help this story would never have come to life.

One

Raiders from the Mist

Sixteen year old Patrick felt the cool tingle of the wet grass on his feet as he strolled through his father's farm on this late spring morning. As was typical for the west coast of Britain, dense fog enveloped all of the hills and farm buildings. Patrick was excited that his parents had let him stay at their country villa while his father took care of business in London. He had assured them that he was old enough to take care of himself and would be just fine. Besides, he would be in the company of their many servants.

As his sandal-covered feet sloshed through the moist green grass, Patrick's thoughts were on horses and his formal education that would begin in a few weeks. Patrick wasn't looking forward to his schooling at all. Nothing but endless drills, memorization, and study. Those things were okay for the bookish boys. But Patrick was a man of action—not books.

"People say I'm an empty-headed dreamer, but they'll see. Someday, I'll be governor of Britain," Patrick said to himself, as he tossed his blond head with an air of importance. He stopped on a grassy knoll and drank in the sweet fragrance of spring. The aroma of the damp, rich earth, laced with the perfumed scent of lilacs, tantalized his nostrils. To the east, he could barely make out the outline of his father's barn. He imagined it to be the governor's palace, where he would live someday. To the north, he could faintly see the outlines of the grazing cows. He pretended they were prize stallions from Arabia.

Turning to the west, Patrick visualized that he was addressing an adoring crowd of his fellow Britons. In the gray fog, he imagined he could see the throng in front of him. He could faintly make out their bodies and faces. They seemed so real. But, of course, he was just imagining things. Or was he? He rubbed his eyes for a few seconds and scrutinized the fog again, hoping it was simply a mirage. However, the ghostly figures were still there, and they seemed to be approaching him.

Suddenly, several blood-curdling shrieks emerged from the fog, followed by the terrifying blast of discordant battle horns. Patrick stood frozen with fear as the phantom figures suddenly materialized from the fog, brandishing swords and spears, heading straight for him. Recovering from his initial shock, Patrick turned and ran as fast as he could towards his parents' villa.

Everywhere pandemonium reigned. Women screamed. Dogs barked. Sheep bleated and ran in terror. Servants blindly raced about in the fog like a flock of chickens scattered by a pack of dogs. Those who tried to resist the armed warriors were mercilessly hacked to death or impaled with spears. Patrick darted nimbly toward the outer courtyard of the villa, his heart beating wildly. He dared not look back. *I've got to make it through the gates before they catch me. Once I barricade the gates, I'll be safe.* However, as Patrick approached the heavy oak gates, he suddenly stopped in alarm. Another band of warriors was already waiting there.

Patrick whirled around to run to the hills, but instead he ran pell mell into a pursuing raider. Although he was an athletic youth, he was no match for the tall, muscular warrior. The man grabbed him by his shoulders and threw him roughly to the ground. Patrick landed hard on his back, and his head fell against a large stone. Everything went black.

When he came to himself, he was in great pain. His hands were tightly bound and his legs were shackled. Several warriors stood around him, jabbering excitedly. A warrior kicked him in the side and shouted orders in an unfamiliar language, suffocating Patrick with his stinking breath. From the burly man's gestures,

Patrick guessed that he was supposed to stand up. Grimacing in pain, he staggered to his feet. He soon joined a long line of pitiful prisoners being led toward the nearby coast. Prodded by the spears and swords of their captors, the prisoners slipped and stumbled their way down a rocky sheep path to a small rock-strewn beach.

The raiders forced their prisoners to sit in a circle on the beach while they engaged in a heated discussion. Patrick recognized the face of Marcella among the hundreds of prisoners. She had been his nursemaid when he was younger. He instinctively sat down next to her. "Who are these devils?" he asked her in a hushed tone.

"Irish," she answered back. "But you don't need to whisper; they can't understand us."

Patrick took a quick survey of the scene around him. Several piles of booty lay on the beach. He recognized some of his parents' bronze and silver vessels in one of the piles. Scanning the faces of his fellow prisoners, he realized that he knew most of them. Many of his parents' servants were here, along with some of their rural neighbors with their servants. "What are they going to do to us?" Patrick asked loudly in a panic-stricken voice.

"They'll probably sacrifice us to their gods," an older woman cried nervously. She was pale and trembling.

"What nonsense!" Marcella scoffed. "They'll only hold us for ransom." Although terrified herself, Marcella instinctively tried to comfort the boy who had once been in her charge.

"No!" one of the farm hands exclaimed angrily. "I've heard tales from the soldiers of how the Irish lock their prisoners of war in huge wicker baskets and set the whole thing on fire, burning the prisoners alive." On hearing this, Patrick's chest tightened and his mouth went dry.

"Oh, be quiet! Can't you see you're scaring the poor lad," Marcella snapped back at the man. Then turning to Patrick, she added, "They may do that to soldiers they capture, but not to people like us. We're not worth sacrificing to their gods." She gave Patrick a reassuring smile. "Besides, they well know that a patrician's son like yourself will fetch a large ransom. So don't worry; I'm sure they won't harm you."

Patrick was glad for Marcella's company. It was comforting to know she would be with him, even though he was sorry for her sake that she had been captured too. "But won't the Roman soldiers be here any minute to rescue us?" he asked her anxiously.

"Patrick, you know only too well that there are hardly any Roman soldiers left in these parts. Besides, these warriors have struck with such lightning speed, they'll probably be gone—and us with them—before the people at Bannavem[1] hear of the raid."

On hearing this, Patrick struggled furiously against his bonds, but he succeeded only in rubbing his wrists and ankles raw and bloody. He thought of his parents and fought back bitter tears as he wondered whether he would ever see them again. He suddenly began screaming at the warriors at the top of his lungs. "You dirty pigs! Wait 'till the soldiers catch you. They'll get every one of you!"

Although not understanding what Patrick was yelling, one of the raiders darted over and cuffed him so hard that he fell on his back. A deep gash on his lip began to ooze blood. The man would have probably hit Patrick again, but he was interrupted by shouts from the other warriors. Motioning the prisoners to the boats, the raiders piled in their loot and abruptly cast off.

Patrick lay huddled in the bottom of one of the boats with a number of other prisoners. Marcella had made it a point to stay with him. The warriors bent their strong backs to the weight of their long, narrow-bladed oars, and the light, skin-covered boat nosed its way through the gray-blue sea. The fog had lifted, and the gulls overhead followed the boats, crying mournfully. Before long, the raiders raised their sails, which caught a brisk wind. The cold ocean sprayed warriors and prisoners alike as the boat moved swiftly and giddily through the Irish Sea. It dipped and pitched

---

[1] i.e., Bannavem Taburniae, Patrick's home village. The exact location of this village is uncertain, but it was probably situated near the southwestern coast of Britain.

wildly as it rode one long cresting swell after another.

His head reeling and his stomach nauseous, Patrick vomited uncontrollably. Several other prisoners did likewise. Patrick lay in the bottom of the ship, groaning. He could feel the skin-covered bottom of the boat undulate with the tug of the sea, like the breathing of some hideous sea monster. The boat reeked of vomit and sweat, and Patrick felt dizzy and nauseous the rest of that long day. About mid-afternoon, the sky turned a cold gray, and a heavy rain began to fall. Patrick looked around the boat for some kind of shelter, but there was none.

"We'd usually be eating right now," Patrick said wistfully to Marcella. "I wonder if the news about us has reached Father and Mother yet. Do you think they'll send a boat after us?"

"I don't know," Marcella said softly. "Let's hope so."

Darkness found Patrick's rain-drenched body shivering on the floor of the boat. Angry, exhausted, and cold, he finally fell asleep as the boat continued its journey across the Irish Sea. He slept fitfully on the cold, uncomfortable ship's floor. Sharp pains stabbed his side where the warrior had kicked him. He awoke several times during the long, dark night as the boat pitched, throwing him into his own pool of vomit. Moving away from the reeking mess, Patrick lay there, listening to the roaring of water, the thrashing of heavy spray, the thundering of the sails, and the occasional navigational cries of the warriors guiding the boat. The misery of his situation seemed to double the hours. Finally, he fell back into a deep, exhausted sleep.

The morning sun finally pried his eyes open. However, the light did little more than reveal the outline of the boat that was his prison. Hunger began to gnaw at his stomach, and his parched throat yearned for water. "I'm so hungry, Marcella," he complained. "I haven't eaten anything for a whole day, and I lost my last meal yesterday morning."

Marcella moved next to Patrick. "I know, dear child. I'm starved as well. But we'll reach land soon, and then I'm sure they'll give us something to eat. Remember, we're valuable cargo to them. Watch and see; they'll take care of us."

When all of the prisoners had been aroused, the warriors gave each of them a ladle of water from a wooden bucket, which the prisoners gulped down thirstily. The hours wore on until at last one of the raiders gave a boisterous shout, indicating he had spotted land.

Patrick raised his head and caught his first glimpse of Ireland. Sheer, black walls of basalt reared out of the water like the ramparts of an impregnable citadel. Noisy shearwaters and puffins nested along the ledges and cracks. Below the birds, the furious sea hurled itself against the cliffs. The water glinted gray and foamy as it whirled around the charcoal black rocks. The air was pungent with the odor of kelp and salt water.

Soon their boat was gliding silently into a small cove, followed by some of the other boats. Several men jumped into the cold, shallow water and pulled the boats onto the narrow beach. The warriors motioned impatiently to the prisoners to get out.

Patrick soon found himself stumbling along with the others up a slippery, narrow passageway to the top of some cliffs. The party rested for a moment once they reached the crest. Patrick gazed eastward across the sea, his blue eyes squinting as they combed the water.

"Looking for a rescue boat?" Marcella asked sympathetically as she caught her breath.

"Yes, I was," Patrick replied, shaking his head in disappointment. "But all I see is cold, gray water."

"Don't fret; we'll all be home soon. I'm sure of it," Marcella reassured him. "Now, if I could only convince myself of that," Marcella thought as she looked away.

After a few moments rest, the prisoners were prodded forward on their journey away from the sea. The pitiful band of captives trekked on, looking like a procession of the damned from hell. They marched over fern-covered hills and through U-shaped valleys until they finally reached their destination at the long house of an Irish king.

At first, upon seeing the palisade fence that circled the king's house, Patrick sighed in momentary relief, glad that his weary march was nearing an end. However, his sighs soon turned to cries of horror. There, hanging gruesomely over the wooden gate were five human heads![1]

---

[1]*Confessio §1, 10; Epistolo §10.*

Two

From Master to Slave

Fortunately for Patrick and the others, their Irish captors had no interest in *their* particular heads. The only heads they collected were those of warriors and kings. The heads of this frightened band of women, boys, and servants were of no value as collector's items.

Several women and children came running through the gate with outstretched arms, embracing their husbands and fathers.

Seeing this, Patrick burst out in disgust, "This whole scene sickens me! Marcella, can you imagine someone welcoming these smelly beasts like they were Roman heroes or something?"

"I don't know," Marcella replied soberly. "Has it ever occurred to you that barbarians might have families, just like we do? Love and family devotion aren't limited to the Roman Empire, you know."

"Maybe not," Patrick retorted, "but it's still different. We Romans[1] have never gone around kidnapping anyone. Our heroes are *real* heroes."

"Really?" Marcella responded curtly, as she brushed some weeds off her dress. "Don't kid yourself. Do you think our British ancestors voluntarily joined the Roman Empire?"

"I don't know. I guess I never thought about it."

---

[1]Since Britain was part of the Roman empire, Patrick thought of himself as both British and Roman—much the same way as persons from Britain today· would think of themselves as both British and European.

"Well, they didn't. My father told me that centuries ago, the Roman legions landed in Britain—killing and enslaving our people. I doubt our ancestors felt any differently about the Romans than you feel about the Irish."

Patrick was about to reply when the warriors shouted to the prisoners, motioning for them to follow some of the servants inside the crude wooden fence. The servants allowed the prisoners to relax while most of the warriors went inside the king's house. The frightened prisoners sprawled on the ground to rest their weary legs. Many of them were weeping. Marcella and some of the others prayed aloud. Patrick screamed at the dark heavens for deliverance until he was hoarse. A pretty, raven-haired maiden sat glassy-eyed in a corner as though in a stupor.

From the courtyard, Patrick and the others could hear the boisterous laughter, exclamations of glee, and excited talk of the warriors inside the lodge. Two husky servants carried a large cask of ale into the house, straining under the load.

"I wonder where we are?" Patrick mused aloud as he gazed around him.

"Believe it or not, you're sitting in the courtyard of an Irish king," one of the captives, a red-faced fisherman, answered.

Patrick looked around him in contempt. The king's dwelling was simply a longhouse constructed from rough-hewn logs cut down from the nearby woods. The roof was thatched with straw. Smoke from the fire inside wafted through the thatch, and Patrick could smell the tarry scent of the resin-rich timber. Dogs and pigs wandered around the courtyard.

"This doesn't look like the house of a king to me," Patrick replied scornfully. "But I guess it befits a king of these Irish pigs!"

A dog came up and sniffed at Patrick's legs. Patrick sent him tumbling with a swift kick. Meanwhile, servants scurried back and forth, some of them feeding livestock, others carrying large jugs of water or wicker baskets filled with grain. Patrick began to look for a way to escape. Glancing behind him, his keen eyes spotted a broken, rusty iron plow laying against the palisade fence.

Patrick thought for a moment about the possibilities. Noticing Patrick's glance, Marcella whispered to him, "What are you thinking?"

"I could rub these ropes against the metal edge of that plowshare," Patrick replied quietly, looking away from the plow. "I think it would easily cut through the rope. I could then make a mad dash through the open gate down to the coast."

"And what would be the use of that?" Marcella countered. "Are you going to *swim* back to Britain? Besides, one of the warriors would probably run you through with his spear before you took a hundred steps."

While Patrick reconsidered the matter, a company of servants brought the prisoners large bowls of porridge and several wooden buckets of water with ladles. After slamming the gate shut, the servants untied the prisoners, while two armed warriors stood watch.

Patrick stood up dramatically, rubbing his sore wrists. "Since I'm the only one here who comes from a patrician family," he announced smugly, "I'll eat and drink first." He took a step toward the food but was nearly knocked flat as the famished prisoners stampeded to the food and voraciously wolfed it down. Somewhat bemused, Marcella exclaimed, "I'm afraid we're all equals here, Patrick." Her brown eyes twinkled.

They spent a whole week in the crude courtyard of the Irish king. At night, they were bound, but their ropes were removed during the day. One morning, right after the prisoners had eaten, a group of warriors suddenly appeared. They made the prisoners line up in single file and tied ropes around their necks. Then they led the pathetic group out of the courtyard to a field about half a mile away.

What a scene met Patrick's eyes! A crowd of brightly clad men and women had gathered in the field. A carnival-like cacophony assaulted Patrick's ears. Men shouted, women laughed, dogs barked, sheep bleated, bulls bellowed, and calves bawled. Peddlers displayed their wares, while wandering bards sang joyful songs, accompanied by the clear and resonant plucking of their harps. The whole field swayed with noise and color.

"What's this all about?" the distraught Patrick asked Marcella, who was ahead of him in the line.

"It looks like it's market day," she responded soberly. "I think we're going to be sold as slaves."

"B-but you said we'd be ransomed!" Patrick protested as he started to panic.

Several men led the prisoners to an empty wagon where a small crowd had gathered. The onlookers carefully scrutinized the prisoners as they walked through the throng. An old white-haired woman grinned at the captives through toothless gums and poked at their bodies with a twisted stick. Numb from hunger, cold, and fear, most of the captives put up little resistance as the buyers examined them. Patrick winced as they felt his muscles and examined his teeth, as though he were a horse being sold at market.

"I'll get even with every one of you miserable beasts as soon as I get free!" Patrick screamed.

Before long, Marcella was sold to a blond-haired woman wearing a richly embroidered dress. Marcella glanced back at Patrick as she was being led away and tried to give him a reassuring smile. Several of the men seemed particularly interested in Patrick, and they were haggling with one of the warriors about him. The dickering grew rather heated, but finally one of the men outbid the others. He was a muscular man in his twenties, with auburn hair and green eyes. The warrior struck the young buyer's open palm, signifying they had reached an agreement.

A kind-faced man with graying locks walked up to Patrick and tried to lead him away by the rope tied around his neck. However, a wave of panic engulfed Patrick, and he began tugging furiously at his ropes and screaming out to the dark, gray sky, "God help me! Help me!"

"Easy there, lad," the kind-faced man said calmly. "No one's going to hurt you."

"You speak British?"[1] Patrick asked in surprise, calming down.

"I should hope so, I was born and raised there."

"Then what are you doing here, working for these Irish pigs?"

"I was captured, just like you," the kind-faced man explained as he tried to lead Patrick along. He then stopped and sighed, "Look, we've got a long walk ahead. Quit struggling, and I'll tell you all about myself as we walk."

Seeing that resistance was useless, Patrick reluctantly complied. Soon the young auburn-haired man who had purchased Patrick joined them, and the three men followed a small path that crisscrossed through dark woods and open, flower-strewn meadows. "What's your name?" Patrick finally asked the man from Britain.

"My name is Cedd," he replied. Then pointing at the other man, he added, "And he's Donabhan. What's your name?"

"Magonus Sucatus Patricius."

"Quite a name! You must come from a patrician family."

"I do. My father, Calpornius, is a decurion."[2]

"A decurion? Really? Quite an important man, I take it?"

"Well, to tell you the truth, my father has tried hard to be released from this responsibility, but they won't let him. You see, he and the other decurions have to pay the provincial taxes out of their own pockets if they don't collect enough from the other citizens."

"Sounds more like a burden than an honor," Cedd observed.

"You're right; it is. But my father tells me that it hasn't always

---

[1]i.e., Celtic, the native British language. Many of the Britons, such as Patrick, also spoke Latin.

[2]The decurions were a group of city councilmen who were legally responsible to administer justice, undertake public works, and collect taxes. However, they didn't actually run the day-to-day government of the city. Rather, they selected a small group of magistrates to carry out the municipal functions on their behalf.

been that way. People used to seek eagerly after decurionship. Maybe it was easier to collect taxes in those days." Patrick shrugged his shoulders. "What about you? Do you come from a patrician family?"

"With a name like Cedd?" he answered with a broad smile. "Hardly. I come from a poor family of fishermen. However, we were all devout Christians, Patricius."

"Uh, you can call me Patrick," Patrick volunteered, beginning to warm up to Cedd. "That's what my friends all call me. Tell me, whereabouts in Britain did you live?"

"I was born and raised near Glannaventa, on the west coast.

"Yes. I've heard of it. So were you a fisherman, like the rest of your family?"

"Some of the time. However, when I was about twenty, I resolved never to marry, so that I could devote my life to Christ's service. Through the help of the church, I obtained a basic education and was eventually ordained as a deacon."

"Really? My father is a deacon."

"Is he? What about you? Were you seeking to enter the ministry too?"

Patrick paused for a moment, looking a bit sheepish. "No, I guess not," he stammered, half ashamed. "You see, I'm—I'm not much on religion. I mean, I guess it's okay for people like you—and my father. But not for me."

The men had been walking for several hours and had just reached the top of a high emerald-green hill. Donabhan paused to rest. Sitting on the ground, he produced some bread and cheese from a leather satchel and shared it with the other two men. With Donabhan's permission, Cedd untied Patrick's hands and took the rope off his neck. Patrick rubbed his sore neck and wrists, relieved to be free of the constraining ropes. Cedd relaxed on the grass, surveying the panorama before them of lush valleys, rolling pastureland, and dark, primeval woods.

"Ireland is truly a beautiful place," Cedd reflected, drinking in the landscape. "It's a masterpiece of God's handiwork."

"No, Ireland is a *prison!*" Patrick countered angrily. He stood up and brushed the dirt off his knees. "Any place that holds slaves is a prison."

"I see. And so your parents don't own any slaves?" Cedd responded, turning around to face Patrick.

"Well, ...that's different."

"Oh, really?"

Patrick sat back down and quickly changed the subject. "You haven't told me how you ended up in Ireland."

"Well, one day I was out fishing—I was about thirty years old at the time–and I got caught in a storm. The wind blew me off course, and in the fog and darkness, I was completely lost. Through God's grace, my little boat was finally washed ashore. In the darkness, I had no idea where I was. However, since my boat was badly damaged, I knew I needed to find help. I saw a light not too far from the shore, and so I followed it to a small cottage. Without thinking, I knocked at the door, and..."

"And you found out you were in Ireland and were taken prisoner," Patrick interrupted.

"Exactly. That was about twenty years ago, and I've been a slave ever since."

"And I take it he's your master," Patrick asked, gesturing toward Donabhan.

"No, he's not my master. He's the eldest son of my master, Milchu." Then, touching Patrick's shoulder playfully, Cedd added, "Or, I guess I should say *our* master."

Patrick's lips tightened at the last remark, and he brushed Cedd's hand from his shoulder. He was still sulking when Donabhan indicated it was time to continue on. After awhile, Patrick broke the silence. "What's this Milchu like?"

"Well, he's a little older than me. For an Irishman, he's fairly wealthy. He's got fifteen or so servants and several flocks of sheep—not to mention a herd of cattle."

"I mean, what's he like as a *master*?"

"Oh, I can't complain. He's not bad at all. I've seen far

worse."

"My legs are tired," Patrick complained. "When are we going to get where we're going?"

"Our master's place is near the Wood of Voclut[1]—several days' away. So you better get used to walking," Cedd answered with a smile. He was determined not to let Patrick's constant whining upset his usually cheerful disposition. The small band trekked on until dusk and then set up camp in a forest.

"Ow! I'm not used to so much walking," Patrick complained as he gingerly rubbed his feet.

Cedd produced some liniment from his satchel and daubed it on Patrick's feet. "This is made from sheep's fat," he explained as he worked. "There, that should help. Don't worry, in a few days your feet and legs will be used to walking. I guess you've lived a pretty soft life, huh?"

Too tired to answer, Patrick lay back on the forest floor. Apologizing first, Cedd tied Patrick's legs and hands before they all went to sleep. At sunrise, he released him, and they continued their journey.

"Don't you just love the scenery, Patrick?" Cedd asked cheerfully as they journeyed through emerald valleys and flower-covered hills.

"All I can think of right now is my own misery," Patrick grumbled, massaging his wrists to restore the circulation. "You know, you didn't have to tie those ropes so tight!"

"I'm sorry. I didn't mean to. But I do have to follow orders, you know." Noting Patrick's downcast face, Cedd added sympathetically. "I know how you feel, being a prisoner in a foreign land. I have to admit that I was pretty upset when I was first taken captive. But I finally realized that being gloomy wasn't going to change the way things are. So I just had to make the best of it."

Patrick made no reply, but simply continued to march on with his head hung low. However, over the next few days, Patrick and

---

[1]Near modern day County Mayo in northwestern Ireland.

Cedd became friends as they journeyed to the Wood of Voclut. Patrick brought Cedd up to date on things in Britain, and Cedd answered Patrick's endless questions about Ireland. On the fifth day, the party began to cross a vast peat bog.

"Help me, Cedd! I'm sinking!" Patrick suddenly cried in alarm, flailing his arms wildly, as his feet sank into the spongy bog.[1]

---

[1]*Epistolo* §10.

Three

Encounter with God

Cedd couldn't help smiling as he grabbed hold of Patrick's arm. "Don't worry, you won't sink deeper than a foot. It's just water and peat. Besides, we're not too far from home."

"*Your* home maybe, but not mine," Patrick shot back irritably as he freed himself with Cedd's help.

That afternoon, the party walked through ghostly gray-white expanses of naked limestone. "Where are we—the end of the earth?" Patrick asked in a frightened tone.

"Well, we may be *close* to it," Cedd answered thoughtfully, stroking his beard. "All I know is that our master lives just over the next hill."

When they reached the summit of the hill, Patrick saw what was to become his new home. He stared down in disgust at the simple round dwelling made of rough-hewn timber, with its straw roof.

"Nobody's going to make me live in a pigpen like that," Patrick announced brusquely, folding his arms defiantly across his chest.

"That's the *master's* house," Cedd replied, somewhat bemused.

"What? Back in Britain, our *servants* live better than that!" Patrick complained in disbelief. He kicked a large pebble futilely as he reluctantly dragged himself toward the house.

As they came nearer the dwelling, Milchu came out to greet them, followed by a great, shaggy hound that jumped up and licked Donabhan's face. Milchu warmly embraced his son and chatted with him for a few minutes. Finally, he spoke to Cedd and had a look at his new slave. Patrick didn't know what was being said, but the master looked pleased enough.

Milchu and Donabhan went inside the house, and Cedd led Patrick to one of the slaves' quarters. This was a wattle-and-daub[1] hut, with one small window that let in air and light.

"I'm afraid there'll be no tile floors here, Patrick, and no soft couches to sleep on," Cedd warned in an understanding voice. "But you're going to have to make the best of it."

"Where—where am I supposed to sleep?" Patrick scowled. Cedd pointed to a pile of filthy straw scattered on the dirt floor.

"Never!" Patrick retorted. "I'll never sleep there."

"All right. Stand up all night if you like," Cedd replied matter-of-factly. "I don't know about you, but I'm hungry. The cook has a meal ready. So I say let's eat and then worry about the bedding."

After supper, Patrick soon fell into a deep sleep, despite his earlier protests. In fact, it was the best sleep he had had since his kidnapping. He dreamt that he was back in his father's villa in Britain, enjoying happy times again with his parents. He slept until the earliest sunbeams found their way through the small window.

When he awoke, he was disheartened to find he was still in his cramped, damp cell. However, Cedd soon appeared in the doorway. With a warm smile, he handed Patrick a chunk of bread and a water bottle. "For a fellow who said he would never sleep on a pile of straw, you seem to have done quite well," he teased Patrick good-naturedly.

"I guess I was more tired than I realized," Patrick replied between yawns. Soon he was following Cedd through the outer gate of the courtyard into the meadow that stretched beyond. They chatted the whole way as they walked through grassy fields dotted with the gentle yellow of buttercups.

"I've learned that the master wants to make a shepherd out of

---

[1]A type of construction using mud and sticks.

you," Cedd informed Patrick.

"Well, I don't want to be a shepherd," Patrick replied glumly.

"Hey, you ought to be excited!" Cedd prodded Patrick, his hazel eyes sparkling. "It means you'll get to be out in the fresh air. Even better, the two of us will get to work together much of the time."

The two men trudged along with Patrick sulking the entire way, until they reached one of the master's sheep herds on a hillside. A boy about Patrick's age was watching over them. Cedd and the youth talked for a few moments, then the young man headed back to the house.

"That's Kilian," Cedd explained to Patrick as he watched the young shepherd disappear over a hill. "He's a nice lad."

Patrick only shrugged his shoulders.

Surveying the flock of sheep, Cedd explained, "Now, the first thing we need to do, Patrick, is to herd these sheep to a fresh pasture." Spying a long stick, Cedd picked it up and continued, "Here, use this to help you."

Patrick folded his arms and refused to take it. When Cedd persisted, Patrick reluctantly held out his hand. He warily took hold of the staff as though it were a snake.

"Well, it's not going to bite you," Cedd chided him, shaking his head. "Now help me prod these sheep, so we can start them moving."

Patrick watched Cedd as he worked the sheep, and he reluctantly began to imitate him. When they finally reached the new pasture, the two men sprawled out on a grassy hillside and rested while the sheep grazed.

"Really, you couldn't ask for a better job," Cedd reflected. "It's so peaceful and beautiful out here. I have to admit it's not so great in the winter, and it does get lonely at times. But for now, we'll get to work together. So we won't have to worry about loneliness, will we?"

Patrick didn't answer; he just gazed into the distance.

"Thinking about home, are you?" Cedd asked sympathetically.

Patrick nodded wistfully. "Yes, I'm thinking about my father's country villa with its soft couches and warm baths. I'm thinking about my friends back in the village. They'll be starting their formal education soon, you know. How I wish I could be with them once more, chasing each other, skipping stones across the creek that runs through our village, and playing catch with a ball."

"That does sound grand."

"But most of all, I'm thinking about my parents. Cedd, right now I would give anything to look once more upon my mother's gentle face and enjoy her loving embrace. I can't tell you what I would give to walk hand in hand again with my father, strolling through the streets of Bannavem or the fields of our farm." Patrick blinked back tears.

"Bannavem? That's your home town? I don't think I've ever heard of it."

"Yes, it's where I'm from," Patrick replied, quickly wiping away a tear. "The full name is Bannavem Taburniae, but I'm not surprised you haven't heard of it. It's just a small village. But it's not too far from Corinium. Have you heard of that?"

"Yes, I'm familiar with Corinium. I understand it's quite a prosperous city."

The two men chatted for awhile, watching the sheep. Finally, Cedd took some food from his pouch and suggested that Patrick do the same.

"I won't be here forever, will I?" Patrick asked apprehensively, tearing off a chunk of bread from his loaf. "Surely the legions will come over and rescue me or something."

Cedd gave Patrick an understanding smile. "Patrick, I wish I could give you hope that they would. But I would only be deceiving you. I've been here twenty years, and the Roman soldiers have never landed in Ireland. Your only hope now is God."

"Don't talk to me about God!" Patrick shouted testily, standing up and pacing. "Where was God when the Irish raided our farm? Where was God when we were all on the beach praying to Him?

I cried out to Him until I was hoarse—but nothing! Just a cold, dark sky."

"And what have you ever done for *Him*?" Cedd retorted, raising his own voice.

Patrick stood there silently, unable to answer. "Well–er–nothing," he finally admitted sheepishly. Then, raising his voice, he added forcefully, "And I'm glad of it!"

"Yet you expect Him to be at your beck and call the minute you're in trouble, is that it?" Cedd looked Patrick squarely in the eye.

Patrick thought for a moment, running his fingers nervously through his unkempt blond hair. "Well, you were a deacon, weren't you? But look at you; God didn't help you either, did He?"

"God never promised us that He will deliver us from every calamity. I don't serve Him because of what I think He'll do for me in this life. I serve Him because I love Him. Has it ever occurred to you that maybe God has allowed you to be captured because He loves you?"

"Because He *loves* me? Don't make me laugh!" Patrick sneered, his blue eyes flashing.

"No, I'm serious," Cedd persisted, standing up and joining Patrick. "I think that God often uses calamity to bring people to Him."

"Well, if that's what He's trying to do, He's using the wrong method. This whole thing has turned me against Him."

"Sometimes that happens," Cedd responded, fingering his staff thoughtfully. "You see, calamity is like the heat of the sun. The sun's warmth hardens moist clay, causing it to become brittle. In fact, it can turn wet clay into bricks. Yet, the very same heat *softens* a lump of wax. Similarly, when God permits calamity to befall mankind, some hearts will be hardened and others will be softened. The choice lies with the one experiencing the calamity. Patrick, you can choose to be hardened by what has befallen you, or you can choose to be softened by it. The decision is yours."

Patrick thought about Cedd's words, but he said nothing in reply. About mid-afternoon, the sheep began foraging again, and they grazed for several hours.

"I need your help now, Patrick," Cedd suddenly announced, arousing Patrick from his pensive mood. "We've got to find a safe bedding ground for the sheep tonight. Where we are now won't work. There's too much brush nearby. It may be hiding predators."

"So what do you want me to do?" Patrick asked in a helpful tone.

"I need you to scout the area to find a good bedding ground, one that's free of brush and large rocks. I'll stay here and watch the sheep."

Patrick quickly scrambled to his feet, glad to break the embarrassing silence. He jogged past the grazing sheep to the top of a nearby hill. From that vantage point, he didn't see any places that would be suitable for the night. So he jogged down that hill and climbed up the next one. From there, he spied a likely place. He walked over to it in order to examine it more carefully. "Yes, this should work splendidly," he said to himself. He then scurried back and described the bedding place to Cedd.

"That sounds like a good spot. Let's begin moving the sheep so we'll reach it about the time we're ready to bed them down," Cedd advised.

Patrick and Cedd slowly herded the sheep toward the bedding ground, reaching it at dusk. Once the flocks settled in, Cedd explained to Patrick that they now had to verify that the flock was intact.

"How do we do that?" Patrick asked with a wrinkled brow, scanning the flock.

"Well, in this particular flock, which I'm quite familiar with, there are eight marker sheep."

"What are marker sheep?"

"They are sheep that are unusual in appearance, such as black sheep or ones with peculiar features—like that ram over there with a broken horn. If any of the marker sheep are missing, you can bet that thirty or forty other sheep are also missing."

Cedd identified the other marker sheep to Patrick, verifying that they were all present. The men then quickly set to work setting up a crude camp, gathering wood for a fire and preparing food for supper. They then enjoyed a hearty soup of leeks, oatmeal, and milk.

"How do you like the soup?" Cedd asked between mouthfuls.

"It's not bad at all. I'll try to get you a job at my father's villa as a cook," Patrick answered with a twinkle in his eye. The two men laughed as they ate and then prepared for bed.

"You mean you're not going to tie me up?" Patrick asked in a surprised voice when they lay down.

"What for? Even *you* have enough sense not to try to run away. You'd never find your way back to the coast. Even if you did, you'd have no boat to take you back to Britain."

"Yeah, I guess you're right," Patrick replied as he closed his eyes. He lay there in his bedding for about an hour, pretending to doze. Once he was satisfied that Cedd was sound asleep, he quietly stole away. In the pale moonlight, he silently climbed a nearby hill and then stopped to rest. He looked back at the campsite and confirmed that Cedd was still sleeping. *I'm free at last!* Patrick now jogged down the far side of the hill and continued through the empty meadow below it. Finally, he sat down on a large rock to rest and catch his breath.

"Where am I now?" Patrick wondered. He looked all around him and then up at the stars. "I wish I knew the constellations, like the sailors. But I don't," he thought, biting his lip. He walked aimlessly a little farther and then stopped.

"Cedd was right," he finally told himself, fighting back tears. "I'm here to stay; I'll never be able to run away. There's no hope for me now." As Patrick slowly walked back to camp, he thought about their conversation that morning about the workings of God. In fact, the conversation had been on his mind all day. Patrick stared for awhile at the moonlit sky and then dropped to his knees.

"Father, please forgive me. I know I have no right to ask

anything of you. I'm really sorry for the way I've ignored your Word. And I know I've ignored the things my parents tried to teach me. But please—please forgive me. I don't want to be a slave here in Ireland." Patrick fell prostrate, his face buried in the damp, cool grass. He lay there for what seemed like an hour, anguishing over his foolish life. Finally, he felt a new stirring in his heart. "Father," he continued his prayer, "if I have to be a slave, let me be *your* slave. Please take away this heart of unbelief and give me more faith. Please, Father. I want to serve you."

Patrick lay there awhile longer, sensing that God was accepting his repentance. He felt a new love for God stirring in his heart. "I've got to get back before Cedd finds that I'm gone," he suddenly remembered. With God's help, he managed to find his way back to the hill overlooking the camp. When he reached the summit of the hill, he paused to rest. He could see that Cedd was still asleep in the camp. "Thank you, Father!" he prayed silently as he descended toward camp.

The next morning, Cedd had to shake Patrick in order to wake him. As soon as he was up, Patrick suddenly blurted out, "Cedd, I need to confess something to you."

"Oh, what's that?"

"Last night, I–er–tried to run away. But please don't be mad at me. It was just as you said; I soon realized that I couldn't possibly escape. In the dark, I couldn't even remember which way was east." Patrick paused for a moment, to make certain that Cedd wasn't angry. When he saw that Cedd was smiling, he continued, "But there's something more. I've been thinking a lot about the things you said yesterday. About God, I mean. I realize now how wrong I've been to turn my back on God. I probably deserve everything that has happened to me. I confessed that to God last night. I've decided to serve Jesus Christ the rest of my life. From now on, I'm going to be *His* slave."

Cedd was beaming, and he came over and hugged Patrick. "I, too, have something to confess," he said. "I was awake last night when you left. I was praying for you the whole time. Now I know

God has answered my prayers." The two men prayed joyfully together and then went to work tending the sheep.

In the weeks that followed, Patrick gradually accepted his new role in life as a slave in Ireland. He still complained, but not as often. One day he cheerfully asked Cedd, "Did I tell you that my father has several herds of sheep at our country estate?"

"No, I don't think you ever told me."

"I never personally handled the sheep, of course. All the manual work on my father's estate is done by our servants."

"So now you're getting to find out what life is like for those servants," Cedd remarked with a grin.

"That's for sure! I know one thing, when I get back home, I'll show the servants a bit more appreciation than I used to."

"*When* you get home? Don't you mean *if* you get home?" Cedd corrected him.

"No, I mean *when*," Patrick answered resolutely. "You see, I have prayed to God to rescue me from Ireland. You said He was my only hope."

"Yes, I did say that," Cedd agreed, putting his arm around Patrick in a fatherly way. Then, clearing his throat nervously, he continued, "However, as I also said, nowhere in Scripture does God promise to deliver us from all the calamities of life. Remember, He allowed His own Son to be arrested, beaten, and crucified."

"So God probably won't rescue me—is that what you're saying?" Patrick retorted defensively.

"Not necessarily. That's entirely up to Him. It certainly is in His power. I just don't want you to get your hopes up too high."

"I see," Patrick answered disappointedly. "How soon will I know if God is going to grant my prayer?"

"That's not an easy question to answer. But you mustn't think that you can just pray one time and expect to get an answer. Sometimes it works that way, but not usually. Do you ever remember hearing the parable of the persistent widow when you were in church?"

Patrick shook his head.

"Well, the parable is about a poor widow who wanted an unrighteous judge to give her justice. However, he was reluctant to do so. So she kept pestering him day and night until he finally granted her request. Jesus wants us to persist in prayer, just like that widow."

Patrick's face lit up. "Then, I'll *be* that widow. I'll keep pounding on the gates of heaven until God is so tired of hearing me He'll grant my request just to have some peace and quiet."

Cedd chuckled. "Well, let's hope so. But we best be moving the flock now. If we leave the sheep at one place too long, they will over graze the pasture, ruining it." The men worked together, herding the flock to a new pasture. When they reached their new site, they rested and ate their noon meal.

"Do you see this plant, Patrick?" Cedd asked, holding up a broad-leafed plant in his hands. "This is poisonous to the sheep. Always keep a lookout for it. If you ever see one of the sheep eating it, chase him away from the plant."

Patrick assured Cedd that he would always keep a vigilant eye for it. "By the way," he said, changing the subject, "I was wondering if you would teach me the language they speak here. I would love to be able to talk with Kilian and the other slaves."

Cedd beamed. "I'll be happy to do that. I was wondering if you would ever ask. The language they speak here is called Gaelic. Point to something, and I will tell you the Gaelic word for it." Patrick pointed to one of the sheep, and Cedd told him the Gaelic word for "sheep."

"How do you say 'sky' in Gaelic? And what's the word for 'God'?"

As the days passed, Patrick learned more about shepherding and picked up more and more Gaelic words and phrases. Eventually, he was able to string together enough words to make simple sentences in halting, broken Gaelic. The work with the sheep and the new language helped to keep Patrick's mind off of home. Yet, he regularly prayed for deliverance throughout the day—and much of the night, too. Spring turned into summer. The meadows were aglow with yellow, white, and purple. The sun hung in the sky well into the evening.

One morning, Kilian met Cedd and Patrick. "Greetings. I'm glad I found you," Kilian announced with a big smile. "Milchu wants you to begin herding the sheep back to the corral. It's time to shear them." Patrick could make out some of the words, but not everything. He then introduced himself to Kilian and practiced some of his Gaelic phrases on him. After Kilian left, Patrick told Cedd, "I understood some of the things he was telling you, but I couldn't follow it all. I know it was something about the sheep. But what?"

"Oh, he told us that it's time to bring the sheep back to the house for shearing."

Patrick and Cedd worked together, herding the sheep back to the main dwelling. At Cedd's request, Patrick then worked diligently to remove all weeds and other foreign matter from the fleeces.

"Will you teach me how to shear the sheep?" he asked Cedd.

"Eventually. But for now, just watch and try to learn as much as you can from observing us. When we're finished, we'll watch the women dye the wool."

"That sounds great."

During the next few days, Patrick watched the other shepherds skillfully shear the sheep. When the shearing was finished, Cedd took Patrick over to an area where the women were soaking the wool in large vats. "Well, as I'm sure you've already noticed, the Irish love to wear bright colors," Cedd mentioned as they were walking. Stopping next to some large iron cauldrons, he explained, "To dye the wool, the women will soak it in these vats of dye overnight. Tomorrow, they'll set the colors with salt and vinegar."

"But where do they get the colors?"

"Oh, from various plants. They get green from moss, red from hawthorn berries, purple from elderberries, and yellow from furze. They boil the vegetation for about a half an hour to get the dye from the plants."

After spending another day around the homestead, it was time for Patrick and Cedd to lead the sheep back up into the mountain pastures. As they made their way back up into the higher grounds, the mist hung like a veil over the countryside, gently blurring the hills and mountains.

"It was a foggy morning just like this when the Irish warriors raided us and took me captive," Patrick commented. "Cloaked in the fog, they made it all the way to my father's villa without anyone noticing them."

"Yes, fog is a raider's ally."

"Oh, did I tell you that I've decided to pray at least a *hundred* times every day, and as much as I can through the night?" Patrick asked Cedd excitedly. "I started last week."

"A hundred times a day!"

"And as much as I can at night."

"Patrick, you really have become the persistent widow. I'm afraid you put me to shame."

"Well, at first it was really hard. But now I find it quite easy. Talking to God is just like talking to you. I'm guessing that by now He's already tired of my pestering Him. But I'm going to keep right on until He finally grants my prayer."

Having reached a good pasture, the men rested while the sheep grazed. Patrick took a long drink from his water bottle. He studied the bottle for a moment. It was made from a sheep's stomach, with an ox hide thong connecting the two ends. The strap made it easy for Patrick to carry the bottle around his shoulder as he moved about. He drew an iron dagger from his belt and cut a large hunk out of the round loaf of bread in his satchel. He gazed at the shamrock-green pasture before him, dotted with sheep like fluffs of cotton. Everything was quiet, except for the bleating of the sheep and the occasional shrill cries of lambs separated from their mothers. The wind whispered mournfully through the mountains.

Cedd finally broke the silence. "How many people were taken captive with you? Do you have any idea?"

"It seemed like thousands to me."

"I doubt it was that many from one raid. But altogether there probably are thousands of British slaves in Ireland right now. After all, the raids have been going on for decades. I wonder if God is preparing Ireland for something?"

"Whether he is or isn't, all I know is that I want out of here," Patrick responded with a laugh.[1]

---

[1] *Confessio* §16.

Four

The Druids

"Have you ever seen a Druid?" Patrick asked Cedd one morning. "From the time I was a little boy, I've heard about the Druids."

"Ah, those mysterious priests of the Irish," Cedd answered as he tied his sandals. "Indeed, I have. In fact, I've seen them many times."

"I never have," Patrick responded. "However, my grandfather Potitus told me that there used to be many of them in Britain."

"Your grandfather was right. In fact, at one time, Britain was the center of Druidism. However, the Romans outlawed the Druids a long time ago. That's why you've never seen one."

"Why did they outlaw them?"

"Because the Druids were offering human sacrifices." Seeing the astonished expression on Patrick's face, Cedd continued, "Well, we best start herding the sheep back home. The master wants his flocks at home for Lughnasa, which will begin in a few days. I venture to say that you'll see your first Druid then. But don't worry, they won't be sacrificing any humans."

Patrick's eyes sparkled with curiosity. "What's Lughnasa?"

"It's one of the main Irish festivals, dedicated to the pagan god Lugh. It falls around August 1 on our Roman calendar."

"I've never heard of Lugh before. What kind of god is he supposed to be?"

"The Irish think of Lugh as a young, handsome man with marvelous abilities. He's not only a god of the harvest, but also a god of war, commerce, craftsmanship, and games. He's probably their favorite god. It's going to be quite a festival. There's always lots of feasting—even for the servants. However, you and I need to be very careful not to get mixed up in the idolatry in any way."

When Patrick and Cedd reached home the next day, they discovered that Milchu's entire clan had already gathered. Milchu's other shepherds were there as well. For a few days, the people enjoyed themselves—feasting, drinking, and playing various games. Patrick and Cedd feasted on mutton, beef, and various soups.

However, the morning of Lughnasa found the people quiet and waiting eagerly for something. "What's happening?" Patrick asked Cedd anxiously.

"Shh. The people are waiting for the arrival of the Druids. Let's get behind that wooden cart over there and stay out of the way."

After waiting for about an hour behind the cart, Patrick suddenly exclaimed, "Look! Who's that coming over the hill?"

"Those are the Druids. It's easy to spot them because of their dress. They almost always wear simple white wool robes. Their only ornaments are gold torques[1] worn around their necks." As the group of Druids came closer, Cedd pointed out, "See that man with the large white beard and balding head? He's their leader."

While the people prepared the great feast for that day, the Druids attended to the solemn duties of thanking the god Lugh for the summer harvest and appeasing him with animal sacrifices. Cedd and Patrick refused to eat any of the food sacrificed to him. When the feast was over, they returned the sheep to the pastures.

As the summer slowly approached its end, the deep purple of heather colored the treeless mountains. Patrick continued to grow in body and mind—and in his faith and love of God. His shepherding skills were increasing, and he was speaking more and more Gaelic. Although Ireland had seemed like such a dark, foreboding

---

[1]Metal bands in the shape of a horseshoe.

place when he had first arrived, he could now appreciate the beauty of God's creation around him. Everywhere he looked, his eyes were dazzled by the vivid kelly green landscape, born of rain and lime-rich soil. Balsam choked the riverbanks. Tranquil lakes, surrounded by fern-covered mountains, mirrored the bright blue sky. That is, when the sky was blue—which it usually wasn't. Yet even in the endless mist and drizzling rain, the landscape took on a mysteriously beautiful aura.

"You know," Cedd mused one afternoon, "The climate here really isn't all that different from the west coast of Britain."

"That's true," Patrick conceded. "However, back home I didn't have to live out in the weather. I was inside a warm house, attended by servants." Cedd chuckled. "Seriously," Patrick continued, "I think it's beastly of Milchu to make us stay out in the rain. Surely, he won't make us stay out when winter comes."

"I'm afraid he will—at least, much of the time. However, we stay closer to the house in winter. And we do get to sleep inside at night."

"Well, hopefully I'll be gone by then," Patrick pondered. "I've been praying for nearly six months. Surely, God is going to answer my prayers any day now."

Cedd shrugged his shoulders and laughed, "Hopefully so, Patrick. Hopefully so."

"By the way, Cedd," Patrick continued, "did you ever pray to be rescued?"

"Of course I did."

"Really? But you're still here," Patrick responded with a puzzled face. "How long did you pray?"

"I prayed for nearly two years."

"Two years! You never told me I would have to pray that long." Patrick's irritation showed in his voice. "How long did that persistent widow keep hounding the judge?"

"Jesus didn't tell us."

"I still can't believe it! Two whole years! And yet God never answered you."

"Oh, but He did," Cedd responded calmly. "After praying for two years, I concluded that His answer was 'No.'"

Patrick was now visibly shaken "You misled me!" he accused Cedd, his blue eyes glaring. "Praying two whole years, only to be told 'No!' In other words, prayer is a waste of time!" Overcome with hurt and disappointment, Patrick walked away, kicking every pebble and stick that got in his way. He was deeply confused. He had put all of his hope in God, and now it appeared that even in God there was no hope. He didn't pray for a whole week after that.

However, one morning Cedd woke up to find Patrick praying again. "I thought you had given up on prayer," Cedd commented with a grin, his eyes sparkling.

"Well, I've thought it over and decided I'll pray for two years like you did. Maybe God's answer to me will be 'Yes.' Or, maybe He won't make me wait two years. Either way, I've committed myself to pray up to two years, if necessary."

As the first of November approached, Patrick and Cedd spent more time around the master's house.

"What's going on?" Patrick asked Cedd one morning. "It looks like everyone is preparing for some kind of special event."

"You're right. The festival of Samain is approaching."

"Oh, another festival. Is it just like Lughnasa?"

"In some ways. But it has its own peculiarities. The Irish consider Samain to be the most sacred day of the year."

"Why's that?"

"To them, it commemorates the creation of the world. In fact, it's New Year's Day for the Irish. Their New Year begins on November 1 of our Roman calendar. However, as you're about to witness, the main festivities occur on the night before Samain."[1]

"Is it a night of feasting and revelry?" Patrick asked.

"No, actually it's just the opposite. The Irish believe that the spirits of the dead return on the eve of Samain and wander through the world of the living. So they're all deathly afraid. In fact, they

---

[1]That is, on October 31 of the Roman calendar.

think if the dead are not properly placated, they can harm the living."

"So how do they try to placate the dead?"

"Mainly by putting out food for them, things like oatmeal, grain, and cheese. We need to be sure to stay inside on the eve of Samain."

"Don't tell me you're afraid of spirits, too?" Patrick retorted.

"No, of course not. I just don't want us to pollute ourselves in any way with what is going on."

Not too long after the festivities of Samain, the damp Irish winter set in, with its cold drizzle and occasional snow. As Cedd had warned Patrick, the shepherds had to stay out on the hillsides with the sheep on most winter days.

"I'm shivering to the bone, my face is chapped, and my clothes are soaking wet!" Patrick complained to Cedd, shouting over the cold Atlantic wind that slapped his face.

"I know, I'm just as wet as you are," Cedd consoled him. "But at least the master let's us stay inside at night. That's something to be thankful for."

"Do you always have to find something to be thankful about?" Patrick grumbled as he walked about, trying to keep warm.

"It's better than always complaining. Listen, when we're back at the house, remind me to get you some wool clothing. It'll keep you a lot warmer than those linen clothes you're wearing. Wool even retains much of its warmth when it's wet."

"Ugh! I hate wool! It makes me itch all over."

"Well, freeze to death then. I was only trying to help."

"I'm sorry," Patrick apologized, changing his tone. "It was nice of you to offer. Sure, I'll take you up on it. Maybe God will help me get used to the itchiness."

Cedd laughed. "Yes, I'm sure He will."

As the days went by, the rain seemed endless. Day after day, it bathed the landscape in a gray mist. The fields were sodden and silent. As Patrick and Cedd trudged through the muddy pastures and tended the sheep, vapor blew from their mouths. They watched the sheep through the lemon-colored light of the winter afternoons, then brought them safely to their pens in the evenings. At night, they lay on the cold floor of the servants' quarters and listened to the howls of wolves in the nearby Wood of Voclut. Although unhappy about his living conditions, Patrick still prayed at least a hundred times a day.

One afternoon Cedd and Patrick got caught outside in one of the many fierce Atlantic storms. However, rather than abandoning the sheep and fleeing for shelter, the two men faithfully rounded up their flocks. Their eyes squinting hard against the rain, they finally led the sheep back home to safety.

Throughout the winter, the men walked over frozen puddles and sloshed through thick mud. One sunny afternoon, Cedd caught Patrick sitting and gazing at the blood-red berries of the holly trees, which stood out against the deep green holly leaves.

"What are you thinking about?" Cedd inquired, catching his breath.

"These berries made me think about Christ's blood that was shed for us. The more I think about it, the more I realize that I've been doing an awful lot of complaining. What He went through for me was a lot worse than herding sheep in the Irish winter. So I've decided, with God's help, I'm going to try hard to look for things to be thankful for, just as you do."

Patrick was interrupted by a flock of blackbirds bursting out of a leafless tree. The two men watched them for awhile. Then Cedd observed, "You know, those birds flying away make me think of how your own soul is finally breaking free from the shackles of sin that have held it down."

To Patrick, the cold, damp winter seemed to last for an eternity. Finally February drew near, and with it, the lambing season. The days were longer now than at mid-winter, yet the damp coldness was just as penetrating.

"It looks like the master is getting ready for another festival," Patrick noted one morning.

"Yes he is. This time it's the feast of Imbolc."

"What's this festival all about?" Patrick queried.

"Well, it's in honor of Brigid, the goddess of flocks and fertility. The festival is supposed to ensure that plenty of lambs are born."

"The Irish certainly seem to have a lot of gods and goddesses. Tell me more about their religion."

"Well, as you already know, the Druids are their priests and spiritual advisors. I've been told that a man must train for twenty years in order to become a Druid. They're the most powerful people in Ireland."

"Even more mighty than the kings?"

"Yes, because it's the Druids who make the laws and act as judges. Even kings must obey them, and everyone fears their magic. The Druids are the only Irishmen who know how to read and write."

"Where are their temples? I haven't seen one yet."

"That's because their temples are secluded among groves of trees. They believe that trees are sacred, particularly the oak and rowan. They say these trees support the heavens and open a path to the gods."

"Really? Have you ever seen one of their temples?" Patrick asked.

"No, I never have. Not that their temples are very impressive. From what I've been told, they're built of wood and are rather modest compared to the Greek and Roman temples of old."

"I see. What else do the Irish believe?" Patrick inquired, narrowly missing a mud puddle as he walked.

"Let's see. They consider pools of water to be sacred, and they say the number three is holy."

"Is that right? What do they believe about life after death?"

"Well, like us, they believe in the immortality of the soul. However, unlike us, they believe that souls wander from body to body after death."

"That doesn't sound very appealing. Do you think they'll ever convert to Christianity?"

"Yes, I do. I can't imagine why God would leave them out of His plans. I've tried to witness to some of the other servants, but I haven't made any converts so far. Maybe you should try."

"Well, I had never thought about that. But—yes, I will. I'm feeling more confident in my Gaelic now."

Finally spring arrived, and Patrick could enjoy many afternoons in the warmth of the sun. The blackthorn bushes blossomed in the thickets. The woods were covered with anemones and bluebells, and the hillsides once again began to wear the golden color of furze. The marsh marigolds made a brilliant dash of color in the wet spring meadows. Patrick marveled at the beauty of God's creation. But he continued to pray to be rescued.

"Get ready for another festival, Patrick," Cedd warned him one afternoon. "Tomorrow, the people will be celebrating the festival of Beltain.[1] This is held in honor of Belenos, the god of fire and war."

The next day, Patrick watched with Cedd from a distance. "The Irish like to combine solemn rites with riotous feasting and rowdy games, don't they?" Patrick observed. "Now what are they doing? The Druids have kindled two huge bonfires, and it looks like they're trying to force the master's cattle into the fire."

"Well, not exactly," Cedd explained. "One of the fires is from oak wood and the other is of yew. What the Druids are doing is driving the cattle *between* the two fires. The cattle won't be harmed in any way."

"So what's the point of it?"

"Well, it's supposed to purify the cattle. Look! Now the Druids are offering the sacred Beltain oat cakes to Belenos." Cedd shook his head. "You know, these Irish are more in bondage than you and I are. We may be slaves to them, but they're captives of their dark, demonic religion. They're in bondage to their superstitions.

---

[1]Celebrated on May 1 of the Roman calendar.

They need deliverance from these things, just as much as you and I need deliverance from our slavery."

"I see what you mean," Patrick agreed. "I'll pray that God will deliver them—that is, right after he delivers me from them!" Cedd threw back his gray-speckled head and laughed. The two of them then busied themselves away from the festivities.

A few weeks later, one of the servants brought a message for Cedd. When the servant had left, Cedd walked over to Patrick. His usual smiling face was downcast. "I've some sad news, Patrick. You've been here a full year now. Milchu says it's time for you to begin working on your own. I knew this had to happen eventually. But somehow I kept hoping it could be postponed."

"You mean we won't be together anymore?" Patrick responded in dismay.

"No, at least not on a daily basis. But we'll still see each other from time to time."

Cedd accompanied Patrick to the flock of sheep for which Patrick would now be responsible. The two men spent the day together. The next morning, Cedd embraced Patrick warmly before he had to leave. As he watched over his new flock of sheep, Patrick reflected on his year of captivity. It had seemed to him as an eternity, yet still no deliverance was in sight. "Father, how long must I stay here as a slave?" he cried out. But no answer came from God.[1]

---

[1] *Confessio* §16.

Five

The Persistent Widow

As the months passed, Patrick continued to improve his Gaelic. Although he wasn't completely fluent, he could communicate quite well with the other servants. One evening, Patrick rendezvoused with some of the other shepherds whose flocks were grazing nearby. He did this whenever it was practical, as it provided a welcome break from his solitude. This particular evening, one of the servants from the master's house had prepared a nice meal over the campfire. Patrick chatted with various shepherds, then noticed Cedd approaching the camp.

"Cedd! How good it is to see you, dear brother," Patrick called out. He ran over and gave Cedd a warm embrace and the kiss of peace. The two men grabbed bowls of stew from the campfire and caught up on their news. As they were eating, Patrick mentioned to Cedd, "When I was first brought to Ireland, I was kept at the house of someone who was supposed to be a king. It wasn't far from the place where Donabhan purchased me."

"Yes, I remember the area," Cedd said as he dipped a crust of bread in his stew.

"Well, my question is, was he the king of all of Ireland?"

"Hardly," Cedd replied, smiling. "In fact, there *is* no king over all of Ireland. From what I've been told, Ireland has traditionally been divided into five main federations."

"Five federations?" Patrick responded. He washed down his stew with a long drink from his water bottle. "What are the names of these federations?"

"Well, there's Ulster in the north. Then there's Connaught in the west. That's where we are now." Cedd paused and stroked his bearded chin as he thought for a moment. "Let me see, there's also Meath in the central east and Leinster in the southeast. The place you were first taken was in Leinster. But the name of the fifth federation, which is in the south, slips my mind. ...Oh, I remember now, it's Munster."

"So then each federation has its own king?" Patrick asked as he walked with Cedd over to the fire to dish out a second bowl of stew.

"No, actually, even the federations aren't ruled by single kings," Cedd explained. "Rather, each federation is divided into two hundred or so *tuatha*. I'm not sure what our word for *tuatha* would be. I guess you could call them clans or tribes. Anyway, each *tuatha* has its own king."

"So then there are a thousand or so kings in Ireland?" Patrick blurted out in astonishment.

"Yes, I suppose you could say that. But maybe I'm using the wrong word, calling them kings. The Irish call them by the name of *ri*. Perhaps *ri* is better translated as 'chieftain.'"

Suddenly, their conversation was interrupted by a fight that had broken out between two of the shepherds. The two men drew out daggers from their belts and circled one another, occasionally lunging forward with their knives. One of them probably would have killed the other, if the other shepherds hadn't stopped them.

"What was that all about?" Patrick asked Cedd.

"Well, I'm not sure, but I think it was over one of the servant girls. As you've probably observed, the Irish are rather hot-tempered people. I see fights all the time. Actually, the master doesn't care if the men fight. He just doesn't want anyone to be seriously injured or killed. After all, slaves are valuable property. That's why the shepherds broke the fight up."

"What if they had been free men?" Patrick asked in astonishment.

"If they had been free men, they would have probably fought

to the death," Cedd replied as he walked back to the log the two of them had been sitting on.

"Are the women just as hot-tempered?" Patrick inquired.

"Perhaps more so. I've seen some pretty ugly fights between some of the women. Everyone in this country seems to think that fighting is something good. I'm afraid they have no concept of 'turning the other cheek,' as Jesus taught. In fact, from what I've been told, in the olden days, mothers would give their baby boys their first food on the tips of their fathers' swords."

"What was the purpose of that?"

"I guess it was so the young children would grow up thinking that a sword is something good. You see, the Irish war against *each other* far more than they war against the British. In fact, the Irish even carry their wars with them to their graves."

"What do you mean?" Patrick asked as he cleaned some mud off of his sandals.

"Well, they often bury their kings—or, er, chieftains—with a sword or spear in their hands."

"Have you ever seen one of their battles?" Patrick asked.

"Aye, that I have. In fact, I've seen several of them. I still remember the first one I witnessed. It was a few years after I had been sold to Milchu as a slave. I was out with a flock of sheep, not too far from where his cattle were grazing. Suddenly, I heard the strange, piercing sound of battle horns, followed by a deafening din. The sheep panicked and ran, and I immediately dashed for the cover of a nearby thicket. Suddenly, I saw a band of warriors emerge over a nearby hilltop. They had washed their hair in some type of white substance and then pulled their hair up to dry into stiff white spikes. They looked frighteningly hideous. I could see that they created the loud din I was hearing by beating their swords against their tall wooden shields. Most of the men had swords, but some of them were armed with spears or slings. A few of them rode horses."

"Did they see you?" Patrick asked.

"No, apparently not. Besides, they were interested in stealing cattle, not hunting down slaves. Most of the herdsmen fled in fear at the sight of the warriors. Those who resisted were quickly slain. Then the warriors on horseback rode ahead of the frightened cattle and turned them in the direction they wanted. It was all over in an hour or so. The men stole about fifty head of cattle."

"Did Milchu summon the authorities when he found out? "

"What authorities?" Cedd roared with laughter. "The Irish have no concept of societal wrongs, as we Romans do," he explained. "If someone steals cattle back in Britain, the owner will normally report it to the soldiers, and they will arrest the thief and recover the stolen cattle. Right?"

Patrick agreed.

"We view theft as a public or societal wrong," Cedd continued. "But not the Irish. They see it only as a personal wrong. It's no one else's business but the person whose goods were stolen."

"How strange," Patrick interjected. "So what did Milchu do?"

"Well, some months later, he and his kinsmen raided the man who had stolen his cattle. They stole about seventy head of cattle from him. Several men were killed in the battle."

"Did that end the matter?"

"No, the man who had first raided Milchu staged a later raid to pay back Milchu for stealing his cattle. The raids keep going back and forth. I'm glad that I'm a shepherd and can keep away from the whole thing. The raiders don't seem interested in stealing sheep, only in rustling cattle."

"That's insane," Patrick declared in disgust. "No wonder we call them barbarians."

"Oh, the Irish aren't all that bad," Cedd replied with his usual smile. "For one thing, they have a wonderful sense of humor and they're extremely hospitable. They're also excellent farmers, shepherds, and herdsmen. And have you noticed what exquisite craftsmen they are?"

"No, I guess I haven't. Since I spend most of my time with the sheep, I haven't really noticed any of their wares."

"Well, tomorrow, I'm going to be accompanying Milchu's son

Donabhan to market. I'll ask if you can come along to help carry the things he buys. Then you'll get to see some examples of their craftsmanship for yourself."

Donabhan gave his permission, and the next day the three men set off for a nearby market, leading some cattle and sheep with them.

"What are the cattle and sheep for?" Patrick asked. "Is Donabhan going to sell them at market?"

"No, not exactly," Cedd replied. "He'll use them to trade for the goods he wants. You see, the Irish have no coins or other money. So they use cattle, sheep or slaves as a medium of exchange. In Britain, an item might be priced at ten denarii. But here, the same item might be priced at six heifers. Something else might be valued at two male slaves."

Patrick was quiet for a moment. He then asked hesitantly, "You don't suppose that Donabhan intends to barter *us* for some other article?"

Cedd couldn't help but laugh at Patrick's question. "No, we're too valuable to Milchu as shepherds. He's not going to trade us for a wagon or something. You needn't worry."

Before long, the men reached the market. Patrick examined some beautiful ornamental glass and silver plates. "These people really are skilled!" he commented. "Look at these intricate designs. How imaginative they are."

"Yes, in fact their goods are prized throughout Europe. Irish merchants sell them in places like Gaul and Spain. I understand you can even find them in London."

"Really? I thought the only time the Irish came to Britain was to raid," Patrick replied as he studied an ornate silver plate at one of the market stalls.

"That's because about the only Irishmen who come to the west coast of Britain are raiders. But most Irishmen aren't pirates. They have their merchants, just as we Romans do."

The men looked around for several hours. Eventually, Donabhan purchased some knives, enameled pots, and various food supplies. Cedd and Patrick carried the bulk of his purchases back home.

The months slowly passed. One morning in late spring, Patrick saw Cedd from a distance and ran over to him. "Do you know what today is?" Patrick asked excitedly.

Cedd thought for a moment. "No, I guess not. What day is it?"

"Today marks two years since I started praying to God for deliverance. You said that God took two years to answer your prayer. So today should be my day."

"Well, just remember," Cedd cautioned, "that His answer to me was 'No.' It may be the same for you, so don't get too excited. Listen, let's try to rendezvous tonight so we can talk more about this."

Patrick prayed and fasted throughout the day. That night, he was rather glum when he met Cedd. "Nothing," he said, throwing up his arms in despair. "God still hasn't given me an answer."

Cedd put his arm around Patrick in a fatherly way. "That probably means that the answer is 'No.' Remember, I told you not to get your hopes up."

Patrick mumbled something under his breath and then went off to bed. The next morning, he was uncommonly quiet at breakfast. Cedd finally broke the silence. "Listen, I need to move my flock, so I can't stay any longer. But I just want to say that I know just how you feel, Patrick. I felt the same way myself when God's answer was 'No.' But sometimes we just have to accept things the way they are."

"No, I can't accept that I'm going to spend the rest of my life here as a slave!" Patrick countered, raising his voice. "I can't believe I'll never see my father and mother again. I don't think that God has said 'no' to me. Maybe He did to you. But He hasn't to me."

"Calm down, Patrick," Cedd coaxed. "I was only trying to help. Perhaps you're right. Maybe God hasn't given you an answer yet. So what are you going to do? Keep praying?"

Patrick thought for a moment. "Yes, it's the only thing I can do. I think God's testing me, to see if I'll continue to pray and fast. So I'll keep on praying and fasting just the way I've been doing."

"Good. Do as you wish. But just remember, His answer might still be 'No.' In all the years I've been here, I've never heard of any British slaves being rescued from Ireland."

"Maybe that's because they didn't pray long enough," Patrick quickly responded. "Or *often* enough. I may seem unrealistic to you, but I still believe that if I keep knocking, God will finally open the door."

The months and years tediously dragged on. Three years. Four years. Still, there was no answer from God. Yet Patrick kept praying and fasting. Now that he was fluent in Gaelic, Patrick often witnessed to some of the other shepherds and slaves. They listened politely but inevitably would reply, "If this Jesus of yours is so powerful, why are you here as a slave? It looks like our gods are more powerful than yours." Although this was discouraging to Patrick, he didn't stop witnessing.

"Patrick, are you still praying for deliverance?" Recognizing the voice immediately, Patrick whirled around excitedly.

"Cedd, it's good to see you again. Yes, I'm still praying for deliverance, and I'm still praying at least a hundred times a day."

Cedd laughed good-naturedly. "You really are a persistent widow. How long has it been now? Four years?"

"Four and a half years, to be exact."

"And you still can't accept your life in Ireland?" Cedd shook his head.

"Well, I wouldn't say that. As you know, when I was first captured, I felt nothing but hatred and disdain for these 'barbaric' people. However, as I've grown in my love for God, I've also grown in my love for the Irish. I've come to appreciate both the strengths and the weaknesses of their culture. I realize now that the Irish love their wives and husbands, their children and parents—just as we Romans do. They cry no less when a loved one dies. They rejoice just as much at weddings and other happy events. They're our brothers. Still, I don't want to spend the rest of my life in Ireland. I miss home; I miss my parents."

"So you're going to keep praying."

"Yes, I'm going to keep praying until God is so sick of hearing me that He'll get me out of Ireland just to have some rest."

Cedd chuckled. "When I first met you, you were a boy. But you've become quite a man, Patrick. God has transformed you from an arrogant, high-born teenager into a man of God, a man who loves his fellow humans. From a proud master, you've become a humble servant. You're a real man of the kingdom, Patrick, and a man of prayer."

Patrick smiled and hugged Cedd. "I think you exaggerate a bit. But, yes, God has been at work in my life. I can clearly see that now."

More months slowly rolled by. Patrick had now been in Ireland for five years. Each time he saw Cedd, Cedd would inevitably ask him, "Are you still praying to be rescued, Patrick?"

"Yes, I'm still knocking. And if I keep knocking, God *will* finally open the door."

And God finally did.[1]

---

[1] *Confessio* §12, 16.

Six

The Escape

It was early summer. Six years had passed, and Patrick was sleeping out in the fields with the sheep. As usual, he had been praying throughout the days and nights. He also frequently fasted. One particular night something unusual happened. During his sleep, Patrick heard a voice from heaven saying, "It is good that you are fasting, for soon you will return to your own country."[1]

When Patrick awoke, he cried aloud from sheer gladness. God had spoken to him! He was going to return home! He sang and prayed throughout the day as he worked with the sheep. That night, he camped with Cedd and some of the other shepherds.

"Cedd, you're not going to believe this," Patrick said in excited but hushed tones, pulling Cedd off to one side. "God spoke to me last night in a dream. He told me that I will soon be returning to Britain."

"Are you sure it was God, Patrick?" Cedd replied, his eyes studying Patrick's face. "It's easy to be misled by dreams."

"Yes, I'm absolutely sure. It was too clear to have been my imagination." Patrick's face was beaming with joy.

"But how–how will God rescue you?" Cedd inquired with a puzzled look.

"I don't know. He didn't say. Maybe my parents have located me and are going to ransom me. I really have no idea."

Cedd thought for a moment. He then smiled broadly and gave

---

[1] *Confessio* §17.

Patrick a warm embrace. "I'm really happy for you, Patrick. So God has finally answered your prayers! Patrick, the persistent widow!" Cedd shook his head and laughed. "I have to admit," he continued, "that I had given up hope a long time ago that you would ever be rescued. I guess you've taught me something about prayer. I'd like to leap for joy, but the other shepherds might get suspicious."

"You're right," Patrick agreed, glancing at the other shepherds. "How I would love to do the same." The two men smiled and then prayed together.

"You probably should start storing up some food, as you don't know what lies ahead," Cedd wisely counseled Patrick.

Patrick agreed to follow his advice. That night, Patrick prayed through much of the night. The next morning, Cedd embraced him warmly before leaving with his flock.

"I sense that I'll probably not be seeing you again. I'm going to miss you, dear brother. I'll be praying for you." The two men stood there, looking at each other tearfully. Finally, Cedd said, "Good-bye, my friend." He smiled warmly at Patrick and then walked off, driving his sheep in front of him. Patrick watched him disappear in the morning fog.

"It doesn't look like I'll be able to rendezvous with the others for awhile," Patrick told the camp cook nonchalantly. "Could you give me some extra supplies to tide me over?"

"Sure," the cook replied, giving Patrick a couple of loaves of bread, some roasted grain, and a few pieces of cheese and salted fish.

Patrick ate from his new food store quite sparingly, so he would have some food on hand for any contingency. Then, a few nights later, God spoke to him once again in a dream. This time, God simply said, "Look, your ship is ready!"[1] When Patrick awoke, he knew this was the day he was to leave. He didn't know what God meant by "Your ship is ready." Perhaps his parents had

---

[1] *Confessio* §17.

come to ransom him. Perhaps a legion of Roman soldiers had landed. He didn't know. But it didn't really matter. God had spoken to him, and that was all he cared about.

Patrick worked throughout that day as normal. As soon as it was dark and the sheep were safely bedded down for the night, he asked God what he was to do. He sensed the Holy Spirit nudging him to rise and flee to the east coast. So Patrick slung his small cache of food over one shoulder, hung his water bottle on the other shoulder, and picked up his staff. Then he quietly stole away—first walking, and then breaking into a light run.

After running about two hundred yards, Patrick stopped, caught his breath, and looked back. He saw his sleeping flock in the ghostly light of the pale moon. He could go back now, and no one would ever know anything. If he continued on, Milchu might eventually catch up with him and punish him severely. But no. He *knew* God had spoken to him, and he trusted God without any doubt. Patrick turned and continued his flight, never looking back again.

Of course, Patrick had no idea of the precise place where he was headed. He simply followed the guidance of the Spirit as he fled. Leaving the meadows, he headed into the dark Wood of Voclut, where the soft beams of moonlight could barely reach the forest floor. But Patrick knew this forest only too well, having rescued sheep from it many times. He found a familiar path between the dense growth of oak, elder, and birch trees and continued on, sometimes running and other times walking. After a long while, he reached a clearing, rested under a birch tree, and gulped water from his bottle.

Across the clearing, upwind from him, Patrick spied a red deer, a buck with a majestic spread of antlers. The buck stood for a moment on a knoll, then darted off. Patrick waited a few more minutes and then continued his journey past the clearing and back into the woods, following the twisted path through the dense forest. His heart beat wildly as adrenaline pumped through his veins.

Some seven hours of incessant hard traveling brought Patrick to the edge of the forest. It was around four o'clock in the morning, and Patrick was ready to rest for awhile. He took another drink of water and ate some bread. Suddenly, he heard a rustling noise behind him. He sat very still, scarcely daring to breathe. Had he been followed? The rustling grew closer, and he half expected to suddenly feel a rough hand on his shoulder. He waited in suspense, and then a weasel darted out of the woods close by and ran nimbly across the moonlit meadow.

With a sigh of relief and a prayer of thanks to God, Patrick continued his flight. The path on which he was traveling now led him to a morass and then to a gently moving brook whose banks were irregular, swampy, and overgrown with dwarf willows. After a moment's pause, Patrick forded the brook and began climbing up a steep, rocky hill on the opposite side. His hands slipped on the muddy incline. In desperation, he grabbed hold of a rock, but he then slipped again, tumbling down the rocky slope back to the edge of the water. Lifting his bruised, wearied body, Patrick attacked the hill once again, and this time he made it to the top.

His eyes searched the moonlit view around him until he spied a small path, which he followed down the other side of the hill. The path meandered through stretches of yew trees and open meadows. Finally, it brought him to the banks of a second river. Here it intersected another path that ran along the riverbanks. Patrick rested and prayed for guidance. Sensing the leading of God, he took this new path, which wandered along in a pleasantly erratic fashion, sometimes close to the river, sometimes up in the hills above it.

When morning began to softly lighten the skies, Patrick looked for a safe place to sleep. He knew he dared not travel during the daylight. Glancing around, he spotted a thicket of bracken on a hillside, about twenty yards from his path. He made a bed in the thicket and thanked God for His promise of deliverance and for the safe journey. Soon, he was sound asleep.

The sun was already in the western sky when Patrick woke

from his sleep. He lay still and listened for about half an hour, hearing nothing except the babbling of the nearby river as it splashed over mossy stones. He used this time for prayer. He knew he was on a journey of faith, and he dared not break communion with God at any point. Parting the bracken, Patrick peered down the path he had last been traveling. He saw no one. So he sat up and devoured a small meal of bread, cheese, and salted fish.

"I wonder what's happening back at my master's farm?" he pondered. "Undoubtedly, by now the shepherds have told Milchu that I've disappeared. He must be furious. Hopefully, no suspicion will fall on Cedd," he thought. Finishing his light meal, he returned the food to his satchel and prayed some more. "Please protect me, Father," Patrick cried out in his heart. "Please don't let Milchu find me. And–please–please protect Cedd from any suspicion."[1]

Finishing his prayer, he peered out again at the countryside around him. "Where am I?" he wondered. "I wonder which clan rules this territory? No doubt, Milchu has already sent a search party out after me." Patrick instinctively crouched down. "Of course," he thought to himself, "I've probably crossed the boundaries of more than one clan during the night. That affords me a measure of safety." He smiled. "I know only too well that the clans rarely cooperate. They certainly won't unite to look for a runaway slave from another clan."

Suddenly, Patrick heard footsteps on the path. Hugging the ground, he peered once again through the bracken. It was only an old, hobbling woman with a crutch stick. Patrick heaved a sigh of relief and smiled. The old woman stopped for awhile, directly across from where he was hiding. "Oh, my aching back," she moaned as she rubbed her lower back, "and I still have so far to walk. Ohhh." With that, she continued on, traveling in the

---

[1] It may seem ironic that God would direct Patrick to run away from his master, in lieu of the counsel given to slaves in the Scriptures. However, God apparently viewed Patrick more as a kidnapped person than as a legal slave.

direction from which Patrick had come. Soon she disappeared over a hill. He now heard only the faint sound of her steps and her stick, along with her fitful coughing. Finally, everything was silent again. A soft rain began to fall.

When the shadow of night once again cloaked the landscape, Patrick ventured out of his hiding place and continued his journey to freedom, moving quickly through the black, silent air. Although this was empty countryside, the flicker of torches and cooking fires here and there told him there were various huts and houses hidden in the quiet places of the hills. Eventually the path took him close to a longhouse, which he surmised to be the home of a tribal king. He heard the sounds of revelry coming from inside the house, and he smelled the sweet, almost buttery aroma of a peat fire.

He traveled nearly twelve hours that night, staying close to the river. He knew that the river eventually should lead him to the sea. When daylight peeped through the clouds, Patrick once again found a hiding place and slept. When he awoke, he prayed, ate a bit, and then waited again until nightfall before traveling. He traveled for another twelve hours that night, then slept in another thicket.

It was now the afternoon of the third day of his flight, and Patrick began feeling considerably bolder. "It's highly unlikely that any word of a runaway slave would have reached these districts," he reasoned. "For one thing, there's no road system in Ireland. And since the people are illiterate, there's no way for Milchu to send a written message to other parts of the country." He glanced around from his hiding place but saw no one. Feeling even more confident, he deliberated further, "Besides, no one I encounter in these parts will guess that I'm Roman. After all, I dress and groom just like the native Irish. I don't look any different. What's more, I speak Gaelic fluently."

After praying about the matter, Patrick took a deep breath and stepped out into the afternoon light. It felt so good to stretch and move about in the daylight. After getting his bearings, he quickly resumed his journey down the river path. It led him by a wood of birches, growing on a steep, craggy side of a mountain that overhung a picturesque lake. The trees clung to the slope of the mountain, like sailors on the ropes of a ship. "Hello, how are you?" he loudly greeted a woman carrying a basket of grain.

As Patrick continued, the blood-red sun began to slowly edge toward the horizon. He followed the winding path up to the rich grassy glades of a forest. Hundreds of wide-branched oaks flung their gnarled arms over a thick carpet of shamrocks. In some places, they were intermingled with rowans, hollies, and yews. The branches grew so closely together that they totally intercepted the level beams of the sinking sun. In others places, the trees receded from each other, forming long sweeping vistas. In such places, the red rays of the sun shot a broken and discolored light that danced on the shattered boughs and mossy trunks of the trees.

Patrick traveled until he reached the edge of the forest, around midnight. Then he slept on a soft bed of moss at the forest edge. When he awoke the next morning, the blackbirds were whistling in the beautiful emerald and yellow meadow that stretched before his eyes. A gray Irish hare darted across the footpath. Robins, stonechats, and larks sang in the trees and bushes. His heart was bursting with joy, and he praised God aloud for the wonders of His creation.

Patrick continued his journey for several more days, eventually covering about two hundred miles. Passing through well-watered valleys, he at last came to an exceedingly steep woods that scrambled up a craggy hillside. It was crowned on top by a naked precipice. When Patrick reached the top, he caught his first glimpse in six years of the Irish Sea. His heart leapt. To his right, sheer black cliffs loomed out of the water. Raucous colonies of gannets, shearwaters, and puffins nested in the ledges of the cliff. Waves lashed the foot of the cliffs. In front of him, the hill sloped gently down to the rocky beach.

And what was that on the beach? A ship! Almost delirious with joy, Patrick raced down the embankment as fast as he could, waving his arms wildly. When he reached the beach, the sailors were quite baffled. Out of breath, Patrick quickly blurted out through huge gulps of air, "I'm the one! I'm the one you're waiting for." The crew only looked at him in silent bewilderment.

"You're supposed to pick up someone, right? Well, I'm the one," Patrick explained.

The boat's captain, a burly man with piercing eyes and bulging muscles, looked at Patrick contemptuously. He then harshly blurted out, "I don't know who you are or what you're talking about. We don't carry passengers. We're carrying cargo to trade in distant places."

"That's fine," Patrick calmly replied. "Let me come along with you; I assure you I will earn my keep."

The captain's face turned red in anger, and he growled, "Get out of here! You're not going with us, so don't ask again."

Patrick stared at the man in stunned silence. He slowly turned away and began to trudge listlessly back up the hillside, fighting back tears as he went.[1]

---

[1] *Confessio* §17.

Seven

Slave Again

Through his tears, Patrick prayed as he walked. "Please, Father. Please, Father, change their hearts. Isn't this the ship?..." Before he finished his sentence, one of the sailors suddenly shouted to him, "Come on back. We'll take you in good faith and you can repay us however you're able."

His eyes still wet with tears, Patrick ran to the boat and climbed aboard. "Thank you, Father," he prayed silently. He was soon hard at work, hoisting the sails, bending his back to the oars, doing whatever was needed. Glancing back, he watched Ireland recede slowly into the mist. "I hope this is the last time I ever see this place," Patrick thought to himself. As the boat moved eastward, the captain and sailors bowed low and began praying to a small wooden figurine of the Celtic god Taranis. They had carried it with them to ensure a safe voyage. So they were bewildered when Patrick didn't join their ritual.

"What's the matter with you," the captain muttered. "Don't you care whether or not you drown at sea?"

"Of course I care," Patrick replied. "But I pray to the one true God who created the land and the sea. I'm speaking of the Father of the one called Jesus Christ." Filled with the Spirit, Patrick now boldly witnessed to the captain and his crew, telling them about the God of love who sent His Son to die for mankind. The sailors only scoffed in return.

Gently tugging his drooping moustache, the captain squinted his eyes and thought for a moment. Finally, he inquired, "Tell me, now, how did a fine Irish lad like yourself come to be a Christian?"

"I'm not Irish," Patrick imprudently replied, "I'm Roman. My home is in Britain."

"I see," said the captain, his eyes lighting up. "And just what was a Roman youth doing in Ireland?"

At that moment, the eyes of all of the crew were fixed on Patrick. He prayed silently for a moment, seeking God's wisdom. He finally replied, "I was kidnapped six years ago by Irish raiders. They took me from my father's villa and sold me as a slave. I herded sheep as a slave for these past six years. But a little over a week ago, God spoke to me in a dream. He told me to get up and leave, for my ship was ready." Tapping his heel against the deck, Patrick added, "This is the ship he spoke of."

At this, the crew broke into laughter. "So this is the ship that will take you to freedom, is it?" the captain asked mockingly. "Now isn't it strange that your Christian god didn't let us in on his plans? Unfortunately for you, we're not even sailing for Britain. Furthermore, we don't help slaves run away from Ireland." Staring coldly at Patrick, the captain then finished, "You may be free of your first master, but you're our slave now!"

This unexpected turn of events sorely tried Patrick's faith. He immediately turned to God in prayer, and felt God's reassuring hand. He had no idea how he would get out of this new predicament, but he was certain that God would be true to His promise. Surely God had not brought him to this ship just to spend the rest of his life as a galley slave. That night, God once again spoke reassuringly to Patrick in a dream, "Do not despair," He said. "You will be with these men for only two months."[1]

The next morning ushered in dark and ugly weather, with rain dripping miserably. For three days, the small ship bobbed up and down the ocean swells, often enshrouded in thick gray fog. On the third day, the sailors sighted the coast of Gaul. They steered for a

---

[1]*Confessio* §21.

small cove and then dropped sail. The sail rippled and glided down the mast until finally it lay shapeless and lifeless on the boat's deck. Using the oars, the men guided the boat to the beach. Once they landed, the men thanked Taranis for their safe journey. A few feet away, Patrick stood with his hands outstretched to heaven, thanking the true God.

The sailors quickly set to work unloading the ship's cargo, making Patrick do the lion's share of the labor. Once they dragged the cargo chests up the nearby embankment, they loaded the chests into hand carts. Patrick was given the heaviest cart to push, yet he put his strong back to the cart without complaint.

Although the captain would not admit it, apparently their ship had been blown off course, for no town was nearby. So the men had to camp that night in a field. They forced Patrick to do most of the cooking and other chores.

"It was sure good of your god to supply us with a free slave," one of the sailors said mockingly, gnawing on a leg of mutton. "He's not such a bad god after all." The other men roared with laughter. Patrick bristled, but then he remembered God's promise.

"No, I won't get angry," he said to himself. "I only have to put up with them for two months. After six years in Ireland, two months shouldn't be so hard to bear."

The next day, the men walked some more, making slow time because of the heavy carts they were pushing. The hot sun beat down on them from the cloudless sky. "Look, I see a town in the distance," one of the men cried.

"Unfortunately, it's too far away to reach by tonight," the captain said. "Let's continue on for a bit longer and then set up camp for the night."

By late morning the next day, the weary band reached the small settlement. Seeing no one in the streets, they knocked at the door of the first house they came to, but no one answered. They tried other houses, without success. Frantically, they began calling out, but all they heard were their hollow echoes reverberating through the deserted streets of the town. In desperation, they burst into one of the houses, only to find it was totally bare. They hurriedly darted from room to room, but could find nothing. No food, no fire, no supplies. They tried other homes, but found they were all the same. The storehouses were empty and the gardens desolate. No people. No animals.

"Where is everyone?" the captain roared. "What sort of trick is this? A whole town that's empty. It can't be!"

Bewildered and discouraged, the tired and hungry men spent the night there. The next day, they followed the road out of town to try to find another settlement. Here and there, they saw small huts on the hillsides, but they found them similarly deserted. Tattered and weary, the sailors wandered around the countryside for sixteen days looking for a settlement, but found none. Weak from hunger, they faced almost certain starvation.

Finally, in desperation, the captain approached Patrick and pleaded, "Tell me, Christian, you say that your God is great and almighty. I know we've treated you harshly. But we beg you now to forgive us." It was the first time the captain had spoken kindly to Patrick. "Please, pray to your God for us. As you can see, we're all starving to death. I doubt we'll ever see another human again."

"If I were not a Christian, I probably wouldn't forgive you. But our God teaches us that we must forgive everyone—even our enemies." Growing bolder, Patrick continued. "It's not too late for you to believe in Him. However, you must turn around with all your hearts to the true Lord, my God. For, indeed, nothing is impossible for Him. Why, it wouldn't surprise me if this very day He sent you more food than you can possibly eat. After all, He owns everything."

Patrick then knelt and prayed with the men. As soon as his prayer ended, one of the men yelled, "Look! A herd of pigs coming down the road!" At first, the men stared in disbelief. Then, they quickly descended on the unfortunate animals. Although they were weak, the men lost no time in killing quite a number of the pigs. They camped at that spot for two days, eating their fill and recovering their strength.

Although the sailors were not fully converted at this point, they never again ridiculed Patrick or his God. Before they left that site, some of the men found a bee tree full of wild honey. In a gesture of kindness, they brought some of the honey to Patrick. "Patrick," one of the men stammered, feeling somewhat ashamed. "That is your name isn't it?"

"Yes."

"Well, me and the others want to say that we're sorry for the way we treated you and laughed at your God. And—uh—well, we just want to say that we'll never make fun of your God again. And—uh—this morning, me and the other men found this bee tree full of honey. Well, we decided that we wanted you to have the first share." With that, the men handed Patrick a bowl of honey.

Patrick looked on the men with compassion and smiled. "You know, you really didn't have to do this. I'm not the one who brought you the pigs. It was God. It's Him you owe thanks, not me. But I do appreciate it." With that, Patrick scooped up some of the honey with a wooden spoon and was about to eat it.

"We sacrificed the honey to the sun, just so everything would be right," one of the sailors innocently volunteered. Patrick stopped with his spoon in mid-air, and then returned the honey to the bowl.

"I'm sorry, but I can't eat any of this honey."

"But why?" the men asked in astonishment.

"Because you sacrificed it to the sun. Why did you do that? Was it the sun who brought you the pigs?"

The sailors stood silently for a moment. Finally, one of them spoke up: "But we have to honor all of the gods, don't we? We believe in your God, Patrick. But we don't want to offend the sun. We've always been taught that honey should be dedicated to the sun. After all, it's the color of liquid sunlight."

"My friends, you still have much to learn," Patrick said, shaking his head. "I realize that you were trying to do what you thought was right. However, you need to understand that there is only one God. You can't worship my God and still worship the sun—or Taranis."

Once again, the sailors stood there silently, somewhat bewildered. "I guess we have a lot to learn about this God of yours," one of them finally ventured.

When the men left, Patrick fell on his knees and prayed. He sensed that Satan had been testing him.

"Patrick, Patrick! Are you all right? We have some food for you." It was one of the sailors, shaking Patrick to wake him. Patrick slowly sat up.

"Yes, I'm all right, thank you. I just spent a miserable night, that's all. Satan attacked me during the night."

"Who's Satan?"

"Satan is the primary enemy of the one true God. He had been testing me yesterday with the honey that you brought me. He was angry that I didn't eat it."

"See, we told you that you should have eaten it," one of the sailors blurted out. By this time, several of the sailors had gathered around.

"No, I'm afraid you don't understand. When we serve the true God, Satan is always angry at us. So it's natural to have him attack us. But God is much stronger. Satan can only do to us what God allows him to do," Patrick patiently explained.

"What exactly did this Satan do to you?"one of the men asked.

"Well, he fell upon me like a huge rock. My joints suddenly stiffened, and I was unable to move either my arms or my legs. I was in agony. As I have mentioned, I knew Satan was doing this to me because I had refused to eat the honey that you had sacrificed to the sun. So I cried out with all of my might to Jesus Christ—the Son of the one true God. Immediately, God gave me a vision. In the vision, I saw the sun in the sky. But then the sun fell from the sky down toward me. I cried out again to God, and then instantly I was delivered from Satan's afflictions."

Later that day, the sailors cooked and salted as much meat as they could carry. The next day they set out once again to find civilization. They wandered another nine days without success. On the tenth day, their provisions once again ran out, and that night they ate the last of their food.

"Perhaps your God has delivered us only to let us starve all over again," the captain complained.

"Have you lost faith that quickly?" Patrick replied. "I know beyond any doubt that God has not delivered me only to let me starve again. And in His eagerness to save me, He is no doubt going to save all of you as well." Patrick then found a quiet spot and prayed fervently to God for several hours. The next day, the crew had journeyed only a few hours before they found an inhabited town. The men quickly traded some of their goods for food.

"We've been wandering for about a month," the captain told one of the merchants, wolfing down his food as he spoke. "But every town and farm we came to was deserted. What's happened?"

"It's the Vandals! They swept through here not long ago—killing and pillaging. So thousands of people fled in advance of them, leaving entire towns deserted."

Once they regained their strength, the sailors traded their remaining Celtic wares for provisions for the return trip, as well as for some of the local goods that would be valued in Ireland. Patrick spent a few more weeks with the men. On the sixtieth day after their departure from Ireland, the sailors let Patrick go, just as God had promised.

From there, Patrick made his way slowly through Gaul, working here and there to sustain himself. When he finally found a church, he fell on his knees and praised God in a loud voice. When he partook of communion that Sunday, he couldn't hold back the tears. "It's been six years since I've been able to worship with a congregation of Christians. I can't tell you how wonderful this is!" Patrick joyfully told one of the deacons afterward. He so enjoyed the company of these newly found brothers and sisters that he had to pry himself away to continue his journey back home.

Eventually, Patrick found his way to the coast of Gaul and boarded a boat to Britain. When he spied the rocky coast of Britain, he was so excited that he was tempted to plunge into the water and race the boat to shore. Once the boat had landed, he accompanied a group of fellow passengers as far as London. He then set off for the west coast of Britain and his village of Bannavem Taburniae. He could hardly contain his excitement as he thought about seeing his parents again. "Won't they be surprised when I knock at their door!"

Bannavem Taburniae was still a week's walk away, but Patrick's legs practically danced along. It was *so* good to be in Britain again. Patrick sang and prayed as he skipped along, feeling certain that the singing birds were sharing in his joy. The blankets of buttercups made the fields seem more golden than green. A stray dog followed Patrick for several days, and he was glad for the company.

When he finally rounded the last hill and feasted his eyes on Bannavem Taburniae, he couldn't hold back the tears. Laughing and crying, he ran the last half mile home. Sprinting through the narrow, crooked streets, he dashed to his parents' house and banged on the door. However, the female servant who opened the door didn't know him.

"Tell Calpornius and Concessa that their son Patrick is here," Patrick announced excitedly.

Somewhat bewildered, the woman gave the strange message to Patrick's parents. "This must be some cruel joke," Calpornius responded. But he and Concessa scurried to the door anyway. Flinging it open, they stood there in silence, as at first they didn't recognize their son. Then with mouths agape, they rushed at him with open arms. For quite some time, they all stood at the doorway, kissing and embracing one another, weeping profusely.

"The son I thought I would never see again is home! The boy I thought was dead is alive!" Concessa exclaimed jubilantly.

Finally, Calpornius ushered his son inside. "Lie down on the couch. You must be tired from your journey," he said. Then, with a clap of his hands and a quick gesture, he directed one of the servants to untie Patrick's sandals. When the servant knelt down, Patrick gently put his hand on the servant's shoulder and objected, "Please, I mean no offense, but I would rather untie my own sandals."

The servant hesitated, not knowing what to do. He glanced first at Calpornius and then at Patrick. Sensing everyone's discomfort, Patrick quickly put them all at ease. With a twinkle in his eye, he remarked with a smile, "You know, it took me nearly six years to learn to untie my own sandals, but I think I've finally got the knack of it." Everybody laughed, and the awkwardness of the situation soon passed.

Concessa then called for food and drink. Scurrying in and out of the kitchen, the servants soon spread a sumptuous meal in front of Patrick. In her hurry, one of the servant girls knocked a tray of bread off of the table. Before she had time to bend down, Patrick quickly leaned over from his couch and picked up the bread for her. The other servants stared in bewilderment.

After his father prayed, Patrick lost no time in enjoying the feast spread before him. Between bites, he described to his parents some of the things that had happened to him during the years he was gone. He told them of his capture, his life as a slave in Ireland, his escape to the coast, his two months with the Irish sailors, and his final journey home. His parents wept softly as Patrick spoke. It was late at night when Patrick finally finished his tale, saying, "I will never be able to thank God long enough or praise Him loud enough for what He has done for me. At the same time, only an act of God could ever make me set foot in Ireland again."[1]

---

[1]*Confessio* §18-22, 43.

Eight

Back to Ireland?

Patrick spent the next few months relaxing, catching up on what had been happening in the Roman world, and getting reacquainted with his friends. At first, he was hesitant to return to his parents' country villa because of the painful memories it might bring. When he finally did accompany his parents to it, he fought back tears as he walked through the farm.

"You must be mentally reliving the horror of that day," his father said softly. The two of them knelt together, thanking God over and over again for His deliverance.

During the next few months, Patrick avidly read the Scriptures. Although few Christians at that time had a copy of the Scriptures in their homes, Calpornius did, since he was a deacon. His Latin Bible was a yellowed, papyrus book bound in goatskin.

"I'm glad to see you take such an interest in the Scriptures, Patrick. Before you were kidnapped, you didn't seem to have any interest in spiritual things."

"You're right, Father. God has done a real work in my life over the past six years. When I was in Ireland, I can't tell you how much I longed to be able to sit and read the Scriptures as I'm doing now."

"That Bible originally belonged to your grandfather, Potitus. Did you know that?"

"Really? No, I didn't. I wish grandfather were still alive today."

"We all do. He would have really rejoiced to see this day."

"I only wish now that my Latin were better," Patrick sighed. "I'm really struggling with some of these words."

"Yes, I can well understand. You missed your entire formal education because of being kidnapped," Calpornius sympathized.

"Yes, that really hurts. Still, I'm glad that I know enough Latin to be able to read at all. Did you know that none of the Irish can read, except for the Druids? Even their kings can't read."

"I guess I hadn't given any thought to the matter," Calpornius replied. "Of course, they are savage barbarians. So what can we expect? By the way, which part of the Scriptures do you like the best?"

"I'd have to say the Psalms. I see a lot of parallels between my sufferings and those of David. The Psalms give me a lot of comfort, particularly since I experienced God's loving provisions first hand."

Patrick eagerly went every day to the morning and evening prayers at the village church. "Before you were kidnapped, you acted like church was a foreign place to you," Petronius, one of the presbyters, commented. "But now you've made it a second home."

"You're right," Patrick admitted. "Six years ago, when I was in church, I could hardly wait for the services to be over. But now I would be content to spend my entire days here. I love hearing the Scriptures read. I love praying with others. I love singing the Psalms."

Petronius grinned. "I'm glad to hear that. You're always welcome here."

"When I'm in church, I think a lot about David's words, 'Oh come, let us sing to the Lord! Let us shout joyfully to the Rock of our salvation. Let us come before His presence with thanksgiving!'"[1] Patrick explained. "Sometimes you don't realize what a privilege worship is until it's taken from you."

"Yes, I'm sure that's the case. Patrick, I'm not the only one who's noticed a change in you. The whole village is talking about

---

[1]Ps. 95:1,2.

it. They remember you as a carefree, proud young man. As someone who had no inclination toward God at all." Petronius smiled at Patrick and put his hand on Patrick's shoulder. "I'm glad for the change."

Patrick's parents allowed him a few months to relax after his return. However, one day they sat down with him to talk about his future. "You're far too old to study under a tutor now," Calpornius began, resting his arm on the top of the couch. "I've asked around, and all the tutors say they'll only accept boys under the age of twenty."

"But you're not too old to work as an apprentice and learn a trade," Concessa added, as a servant combed her hair. "Once you've mastered a trade, you can think about marriage and raising a family. Rest assured that your father and I will give you all the help you need to put your life back together again."

Patrick smiled at his parents. "Thank you so much for your love. Actually, I've been thinking about all those things myself. However, let me think and pray about it some more, and perhaps in two or three days we can talk again. Would that be all right?"

His parents assured him it would be fine. That night, before going to bed, Patrick prayed at length about his future. "Father, I'm at the crossroads of my life. Please give me direction. What would you have me do?" During the night, God answered his prayer through another dream. Unlike the others, this dream left Patrick shaking. The next morning, he reluctantly told his parents about the dream.

"In my dream, I saw Victoricus," he began.

"You mean the old hermit?" Calpornius asked.

"Yes, the very one. Anyway, in my dream, Victoricus was coming from Ireland on a boat, with a heavy leather satchel slung over his shoulder."

"What was in the satchel?" Concessa asked, leaning forward in her chair.

"I'm getting to that in a minute," Patrick explained. "Now, in the dream, Victoricus walked to our house, knocked at the door, and asked for me. You, father, invited him inside. When I came into the room, he laid the satchel down at my feet. Naturally, I opened the satchel to see what was in it. To my surprise, it was full of letters."

"Letters?" Concessa interjected. "From whom?"

"They were letters from people in Ireland."

"But I thought you told me the Irish can't read or write!" Calpornius objected.

"That's right. They can't. But you know how dreams are. They don't always fit reality. But please let me finish. In the dream, Victoricus handed me one of the letters. At first, I hesitated to open it. But then I broke the wax seal and began to read the letter aloud. It began, 'The voice of the Irish...' Strangely, as I continued to read, I felt like I was hearing the voices of all of the men and women I knew back in Ireland. Eventually, their voices drowned out my own voice as I was reading.

"What were the people saying?" Concessa asked anxiously.

"They were all saying, as with one voice, 'We beg you, young man, come and walk among us again.'[1] At that point, I was so shaken that I couldn't read any further. Then I awoke with a start. I looked around the darkened room and realized that it had only been a dream. Yet, I know beyond any doubt that this was a dream sent by God."

"How can you know that?" Calpornius disputed, jumping up from his chair.

"Because He's sent me dreams before. If it were not for His dreams, I wouldn't be standing here in front of you right now." Patrick then looked his parents squarely in their eyes and said, "God wants me to return to Ireland."[2]

---

[1] *Confessio* §23.

[2] Ibid.

Nine

The Door Is Closed

"Return to Ireland? Absolutely not!" Calpornius was quite angry. "Haven't you suffered enough in Ireland already? Do you expect us to believe that God delivered you from Ireland only to send you right back? What will your master do when he discovers that you've returned?"

At this point, Patrick's mother completely broke down, wailing so pathetically that even Patrick was moved to tears. "Dear God, no, don't let this happen!" she lamented loudly. "Please don't let our boy leave us ever again."

"Think of what the Scriptures teach," Calpornius reminded Patrick sternly. "They tell you to honor your father and your mother. You certainly won't be honoring us if you do such a foolish thing as going back to Ireland. This time, you'll probably be killed."

"Why would God want you to go back to Ireland?" Patrick's mother pleaded. "He saved you from the Irish. Use your head, Patrick. Use your head!"

"My *head* tells me not to go. But my *heart* tells me that I must," Patrick replied firmly. He paced around the room for a moment and then stepped outside into the walled patio. His parents followed him outside. "Look, do you think this is something that *I* want?" Patrick asked, turning to face his parents. "I have no desire whatsoever to set foot in Ireland again. In fact, I was looking forward to having a family and living here in Bannavem for the rest of my life. I'm sure that nothing but hardships await me in Ireland—and maybe death."

"So then tell God, 'No,'" Calpornius insisted.

"But I owe God my life; I'm His bond-servant. I can't refuse Him. As for the reason why God wants me to go back, I'm sure it's to bring the good news of Jesus Christ to the Irish people."

Then, speaking very tenderly, Patrick continued, "I know that the Scriptures tell us to honor our father and mother. But Jesus also tells us that 'he who loves father or mother more than Me is not worthy of Me.' I have no desire to leave you—ever. But I have to obey my Lord."

Patrick's mother broke into loud wails. Even many of the servants, who had been listening in on the conversation, were crying. Finally, Calpornius interjected quietly, "Will you do this one thing for us, Patrick? Will you talk to the presbyters of the church? See what they have to say. After all, God speaks through the church as well as through dreams."

Patrick thought for a moment, gazing into his father's gray-blue eyes. Finally, he replied, "Yes, I will talk to the leaders of the church and see what they say."

The next Sunday, after the morning worship service, Patrick and Calpornius sat down with the presbyters in a quiet room off of the nave of the church. The presbyters listened attentively to Patrick's account of his recent dream and the earlier dreams in Ireland. When Patrick finished, they asked Calpornius what he thought about the matter. After hearing his thoughts, Petronius told Patrick, "Give us some time to pray and talk about this. We'll meet back with you on Tuesday morning. How does that sound?" Patrick agreed, and he and his father silently walked home together.

During the rest of that day and the next, a visitor would have thought that there had just been a funeral at Calpornius' home. Everyone was abnormally quiet, including the servants. No one spoke any further about Patrick's dream. Patrick's parents prayed ardently that God would not take their boy to Ireland. Patrick prayed just as ardently that God would reveal His will to his parents and to the leaders of the church. Everyone waited anxiously for Tuesday morning.

"Patrick, I know you're not going to like what we're about to tell you," Petronius began. Patrick's heart sank. "We're all very impressed by your sincerity and your desire to do God's will," he continued. He glanced at the other presbyters, who all nodded in agreement. "However, God has not made it plain to any of us that this is what He wants you to do. We feel that if this were His will, he would have revealed that to us as well."

"Patrick, this mission is just too dangerous," another presbyter interjected. "Word would almost certainly reach your former master that you had returned. Before very long, you'd be a slave again—if you're fortunate. You might end up being tortured or sacrificed to one of their gods."

Before Patrick had a chance to say anything, Hosius, another presbyter, chimed in, "Patrick, we don't want to hurt your feelings, but you've always been somewhat of a dreamer. We remember when you were a boy you used to dream about being the emperor someday. You were always imagining things. We think this just may be something else you've imagined."

"Did I imagine the dream in Ireland when God told me my ship was waiting for me?" Patrick retorted, raising his voice. His face was flushed with anger. "Did I imagine the dream when God told me that I would be free from the Irish sailors in sixty days?"

"Well, we don't know about those things. But if it was God who saved you from the Irish, He would hardly be sending you back to certain captivity or death, now would He?" Hosius answered. "Besides, the hearts of the Irish are far too hardened at the present time to ever receive the Gospel. They still offer human sacrifices to their demon-gods! Perhaps someday God will send someone to preach the Gospel to them. But, Patrick, you're hardly qualified for such a monumental task."

"That's right," Petronius added in a gentle voice. "Patrick, through no fault of your own, you've missed out on your education. You know none of the canons and doctrines of the Gospel.

You read the Latin Scriptures only with difficulty. For such a task as bringing the Gospel to Ireland, God needs someone who has much more training than you have. When God raises up that man, perhaps you can accompany him. If this dream was from God, no doubt that's what He meant."

Blinking back tears, Patrick left the meeting with his head hung low. He made only half-hearted jabs at his food that evening, and he went to bed early. The next day, Patrick went to visit Victoricus, who lived alone in a simple hut in the woods. Although he came from a middle class family, Victoricus had spent his life as an ascetic man of prayer. Many Christians in the community viewed Victoricus as a prophet; others thought he was just a demented old man.

Victoricus warmly welcomed Patrick inside his hut. "Are you the one I've heard about? The young man whom God delivered from Ireland?" Victoricus' big smile revealed several missing teeth.

"Yes, I'm the one."

"But you look so troubled, lad. I would think you would be leaping about joyfully. What's burdening you?"

"I don't know where to start," Patrick murmured.

"Well, start with your kidnapping," Victoricus suggested, as he handed Patrick a cup of water.

So Patrick told him about his kidnapping, his years in Ireland, and his providential deliverance. "But the reason I've come to talk with you is because of a dream I had last week. In the dream you came to my house with a satchel of letters from Ireland."

"Me? *I* came to your house from Ireland? But Patrick, I've never been in Ireland," Victoricus objected.

"Yes, but dreams don't always fit life as we know it, isn't that true?"

Victoricus thought for a moment. "Yes, it's true. But imagine *me* being in one of your dreams," he chuckled. "We hardly know each other."

"That convinces me all the more that the dream was from God.

You're the most spiritual man in these parts. That's why God put you in my dream."

"You mean, I'm the craziest man in these parts," Victoricus protested with a grin. "But go on. What did the letters say?"

Patrick went on to describe the rest of the dream. He then told Victoricus how his parents responded and what the presbyters had said.

"So the presbyters don't think you're qualified to be a missionary, do they?" Victoricus commented, stroking his long white beard. "The truth of the matter is that it would be hard to find anyone in the entire world right now who is as qualified for this mission as you are, Patrick."

"You really think so?" Patrick answered in surprise. "Why do you say that? You hardly know me."

"I don't have to know you," Victoricus responded as he refilled Patrick's cup. "I've heard your life's account, and I know the ways of God. Don't you realize, Patrick, that you've just graduated from God's training school? For six years, God has been specifically training you for the very purpose of bringing the Gospel to the Irish."

"I never thought of that," Patrick replied, his eyes suddenly lighting up. "But none of the presbyters think I'm qualified."

"Well, let's go over some of the qualifications that the man who takes Christianity to Ireland must have," Victoricus suggested. "And then we'll see where you stand."

"All right."

"First of all, before a man can bring the Gospel to others, he must have a deep, personal relationship with God, marked by a life of continual prayer. Where do you stand there?"

"I guess I'm on safe ground there," Patrick replied. "I pray around the clock. When I was in Ireland, I prayed at least a hundred times a day."

"Yes, I remember your telling me that. Now, the second qualification for the man who takes the Gospel to Ireland is that he must love the Irish people. Do you really love the Irish, Patrick?

Or, deep inside do you still resent them for what they did to you?"

Patrick was silent for several seconds. Then, nodding his head, he replied confidently, "I can honestly say that I love the Irish. Now, mind you, I didn't at first. After they kidnapped me, I hated them. But over the years, through God's grace, I have came to love them. They are truly like sheep without a shepherd. They need the saving message of the Gospel."

"I was hoping that's what I would hear," Victoricus said with a warm smile as he stood up. "Come and walk with me in the woods for awhile. I need to stretch my legs. We can talk further as we walk."

As the two men rambled through the woods, Victoricus continued, "Now, the third qualification is that you must have an unshakable faith in God's sustaining grace to preserve you through any trials. You must have absolute faith in Him to provide for your needs—regardless of the circumstances. Do you have such faith, Patrick."

"I know this must sound boastful," Patrick said with considerable hesitation. "But I can honestly say that I do. I've had to depend absolutely upon him all of these past six years. Yes, I truly believe that He will sustain my needs if I go back to Ireland."

"I sense you have such faith, Patrick. But another thing is that the man who evangelizes Ireland must be ready to lay down his life for the Irish. If you go to Ireland at God's call, you might not ever come back. Are you prepared for that?"

Patrick thought for a moment, absently toying with a flower he had picked. "Yes, I truly am. I've thought about that very thing over the past week. I'm ready to die in Ireland."

Victoricus smiled broadly, then put his arm around Patrick. "Yes, you're God's chosen man for Ireland. There's no doubt in my mind. It's been many years since I've seen a young man with your faith."

"So will you talk to the presbyters for me?" Patrick inquired anxiously.

Victoricus shook his bald head. "I would be happy to, if I

thought it would do any good. But most of them think I'm just an eccentric old man. Anyway, there are some other things we need to explore. We've talked about the important ones—the spiritual qualifications. I'm convinced you're God's man, all right. But that doesn't mean that you're ready to go right now. There are some practical qualifications you must have as well."

"Such as?"

"Well, to begin with, to take the Gospel to the Irish, you've got to be able to speak their language. Can you do that?"

"Yes, I'm fluent in their language."

"Yes, I suppose so, living there six years. But are you mentally and physically prepared for the hardships ahead? You say you're from a patrician family. Are you going to be able to endure hunger, cold, nakedness, and the many other hardships ahead of you?"

"Without a doubt!" Patrick responded immediately. "I'm sure that's why God had me working as a slave for so long—so I'd be ready for such hardships. When I was in Ireland, I was often cold and hungry. I learned how to sleep on the ground or on a pile of dirty straw. I learned to work out in the rain, even in winter."

"Good!" Victoricus responded, clapping his hands together. "Now, what about your knowledge of Scripture?"

Patrick's face went blank and the fire disappeared from his eyes. "I have to admit that I don't know the Scriptures very well," he confessed reluctantly. "I've only been reading them for a few months. I didn't have the Scriptures in Ireland."

"Hey, don't get discouraged again," Victoricus urged Patrick, as he put his arm around him. "Just because God's called you to Ireland doesn't mean that He wants you to leave tomorrow. He's invested six years in you already. He won't mind waiting another year or so for you to learn the Scriptures. And don't be in such a hurry that you run ahead of God. After all, you're going to need to know the Scriptures backward and forward if you're going to teach God's ways to the Irish. You can't get by on just a few months worth of reading."

"I suppose you're right," Patrick said in a small voice, dropping the flower he had been holding. "What else am I lacking?"

"The other thing you're lacking is that you need to go to Ireland with the blessing and authority of the church. Even Paul didn't embark on his journeys of his own accord. Rather, he was sent out by the church in Antioch."

Patrick's face went pale, and he swallowed hard. Sensing Patrick's discouragement, Victoricus quickly added, "There's no reason to feel dejected. You're still quite young. Once you've studied the Scriptures in depth and know the teachings of the Gospel, no doubt God will put it in the hearts of the presbyters to send you. Remember, you've got to wait on God's timing, Patrick. In the meantime, I'll be praying for you every day."

Patrick thanked Victoricus for his godly counsel. They returned to Victoricus' hut and enjoyed a simple meal of bread and water. Patrick was feeling more encouraged now. "I *will* learn the Scriptures backward and forward," he called to Victoricus as he walked away from his hut. "Wait and see!"

"I'm sure you will. Come back any time to see me, dear lad," Victoricus shouted back, waving good-bye.

That night in his sleep, Patrick heard the voices of the Irish once again calling to him. In his dream, Patrick cried out to God, but the words were not his own. It was as though someone else were praying through his mouth. When the prayer ended, Patrick heard a voice from above, saying, "The One who has laid down His life for you—it is He who speaks in you."[1] Patrick woke up, full of joy.

For the next few nights, Patrick experienced the same type of prayer several times in his dreams. He decided to tell Victoricus about these dreams, to see what insights he might have.

"I'm not sure how to describe it," he told Victoricus. "In a sense it's me praying, but the words are not of my own compos-

---

[1] *Confessio* §24.

ing. It's like they're coming from a greater Power within me."

"Yes, it's the Spirit who is praying through you and interceding on your behalf. The Scriptures speak about this. Let me show you." Victoricus produced a well-worn copy of Scriptures from his bedside and turned in them to Paul's epistle to the Romans. "Here," he said, handing the Scriptures to Patrick. "Read the passage that begins right here." His gaunt finger pointed to the passage.

Patrick eagerly took the ragged book and began reading: "Likewise the Spirit also helps in our weaknesses. For we do not know what we should pray for as we ought, but the Spirit Himself makes intercession for us with groanings which cannot be uttered. Now He who searches the hearts knows what the mind of the Spirit is, because He makes intercession for the saints according to the will of God."[1] On reading these words, Patrick's heart leapt. So it was the Spirit praying on his behalf! Patrick had not known what to pray for, but the Spirit did.

"Go and speak to the presbyters again, Patrick," Victoricus urged him. "Perhaps these Spirit-composed prayers have changed their hearts. Meanwhile, I'll be praying for you as well."

The next Sunday, after Petronius dismissed the congregation, Patrick went up to him and brought up the subject of Ireland again. He told Petronius that God was continuing to call him to Ireland in his dreams. He then described how the Spirit had been praying through him. Petronius listened with serious interest and then summoned the other leaders over to hear what Patrick was relating.

When Patrick finished, Petronius spoke up: "Brothers, I don't know whether Patrick's dreams are genuine or not. But this past week, I've been reconsidering the whole matter. Perhaps God is really calling Patrick to Ireland. We can't deny that He did rescue him from slavery there. We need to be quite cautious here, or we may find ourselves opposing the will of God."

---

[1]Rom. 8:26, 27.

The other presbyters nodded their heads in agreement. "Yes, I've been re-thinking the matter myself," one of them chimed in.

Petronius then asked Patrick to wait as he and the other leaders discussed the matter alone in a nearby room. Later, returning with the other presbyters, Petronius told Patrick, "The other leaders and I have decided that if it's God's will that you go to Ireland, then the church in Britain will send you there to do the work of God." Patrick's face was beaming. *The Spirit has changed their hearts!* "At the same time," Petronius continued, "you're hardly ready to embark on such an important assignment right now. You're not even a deacon yet, and you know very little about Scripture, doctrine, or the canons of the church. So the church will first train you in the Scriptures, the doctrines of the Gospel, and canon law. We will not send you out until you have at least been ordained as a presbyter."

Patrick was a little disappointed about the conditions the leaders had attached to their permission, but he remembered Victoricus' counsel not to run ahead of God. He certainly didn't want to be a maverick, operating outside the authority of the church.

After a long pause, Patrick finally responded, "Yes, I can see the wisdom in what you're saying. If it's all right, I would like to begin studying for ordination right away. The presbyters told him he could begin his training in a week. Patrick thanked them and quickly excused himself, his heart bursting with joy. He practically ran to Victoricus' hut to tell him the good news.

Naturally, his parents weren't overjoyed when they heard the news. In fact, the next day, they went and talked to the presbyters about the matter. "Don't fret about this," one of the men reassured them. "It will take many years for Patrick to receive the necessary training. By then, he'll probably have changed his mind. My guess is that in a few years, Patrick will be married, have a family, and forget all about Ireland."[1]

---

[1] *Confessio* §24, 25, 46.

Ten

How Long, Oh Lord?

Within a few days, the entire village knew about Patrick's plans to go back to Ireland. Men would shake their heads when Patrick walked by, and old ladies would whisper to each other, pointing bony fingers at the young man. They all thought he was a little crazy. Though Patrick had been spiritually transformed during the years he had been away, the people in his village had not. For the most part, they were still the same nominal Christians they had been before. They couldn't possibly understand why anyone would want to undertake such a dangerous mission.

"The boy is absolutely insane!" they would say to one another. "Imagine him treating his parents that way, not caring if he breaks their hearts."

Even Patrick's boyhood friends didn't like his transformation. "So you're going to convert the Irish, are you? You'd have more success trying to convert a herd of cattle!" they would laugh. Pointing to their heads, they jeered, "You must be a little insane. But I suppose living six years among those barbarians would make anyone crazy."

Although the insults and ridicule hurt, Patrick brushed them aside and focused on his studies. As he grew in his knowledge of Scripture, he also grew even closer to God. For now he knew God not only experientially, but also through His revealed Word.

During this period, a young man his age named Marcus befriended him. He was one of the more spiritual young men in the village. Patrick had known him before going to Ireland, but back then he saw Marcus as being too "pious" to be any fun. Now he saw Marcus in a different light, and he and Marcus often prayed and read Scripture together. They even confessed their sins to one another. One day Patrick spoke to Marcus in private. "Marcus, for some time now, we've been confessing our sins to one another. However, I've held back from telling you about one certain sin. It's–a–very serious sin. I committed it when I was only fifteen. At that time in my life, I neither knew God nor hardly believed in Him." He continued, confessing his sin[1] to Marcus. The two men wept and prayed together.

If only Patrick had known what impact his confession would have years later, he might have never told anyone about it.

"Here, I thought my training for the ministry would be a quick process," he told Marcus one day as they sat at Patrick's desk. "But now I'm finding out quite differently. It's been an entire year since God called me to return to Ireland. I'm eager to go, but the leaders won't send me since I haven't finished my studies."

Marcus paused from his reading and gave Patrick an understanding smile. "Don't worry," he consoled his friend. "You remember how long God made you wait in Ireland before rescuing you. Give Him time."

"Yeah, I guess in comparison a year isn't too bad," Patrick admitted reluctantly. "But surely He won't make me wait six whole years again. I don't think I would have the patience to go through such a long wait again."

"I'm sure He won't," Marcus agreed. "By the way, how are your studies progressing?"

"I've made great progress in learning the Scriptures; I really enjoy studying them. And my Latin keeps improving each month. However, to be honest, I'm having a difficult time focusing on theology. The presbyters are pretty disappointed in my progress in

---

[1]Patrick doesn't specify what his sin was. Whatever it was—theft, idolatry, or sexual immorality—it was quite a serious matter.

that area."

"But surely you've learned the basic doctrines of the church by now?" Marcus responded.

"Well, I've memorized the Nicene Creed, and I think I have a fairly good grasp of the fundamentals expressed in it. But I guess that's about all that I've learned in the way of theology," Patrick admitted. Marcus shook his head.

"How are *your* studies coming?" Patrick quickly asked, changing the subject.

"They're coming along well. Perhaps we'll be ordained as deacons at the same time."

"The way it looks, you'll probably be ordained *before* me," Patrick responded dejectedly.

Another year slowly passed by, and Patrick and Marcus were finally ordained as deacons. However, the church leaders told Patrick that he needed much more training and experience before he could be ordained as a presbyter or sent to Ireland. Trying hard not to lose his faith, he continued to cry out to the Lord. "How long, oh Lord? How long?"

Patrick realized he needed to keep his Gaelic active, so he would occasionally journey with his father to London. There, Irish merchants displayed their fine Celtic wares and sold cattle and grain. Patrick eagerly witnessed to the Irish merchants and seamen in their native Gaelic. Through this, he made a few converts to Christ and kept his Gaelic from getting rusty.

However, Patrick's mission to the Irish was of little concern to most Britons. They had more pressing national concerns to think about. "I think the end of the world is at hand!" Calpornius glumly told his family one day after returning from a meeting in London. Collapsing in a chair, he continued, "If not, it's at least the last days of Roman Britain."

"What is it?" Concessa cried in alarm.

"Well, as you know, all of the Roman legions have been gone from Britain for years now. I've just returned from London, where

I heard reports that the Picts and Scots are pouring over Hadrian's Wall in the north—pillaging, raping, and killing at will. Irish ships continue to raid the west coast of Britain, taking more of our people as slaves. Now Saxon raiders are plundering the eastern shores of Britain. No place is safe any longer."

"I don't think I've ever heard of the Saxons," Patrick replied with a wrinkled brow. "Who are they?"

"I don't know very much about them myself," Calpornius admitted, throwing up his arms. "They're one of the Germanic tribes from Europe. From what I hear, they're even more cruel than the Scots and Picts."

"Dear Lord, help us!" Concessa gasped, clutching her heart. "What are we going to do?"

"I don't know. We're all at a loss," Calpornius confessed, shaking his gray head. "That's what the meeting in London was all about. All of the remaining administrators and city councilmen throughout Britain were there. At the council, we discussed the fact that when we Britons became Christians years ago, we laid down our swords. Since then, we've had the Roman legions here to defend us. As a result, we've become a rather passive people."

"Did the council come up with any solution?" Patrick queried.

"Yes. We sent an urgent message of appeal to Emperor Honorius, pleading for help. We're hoping to get a fresh supply of troops within weeks."

Several months passed without any word from Rome. One evening, Calpornius came home with a dejected face. "What is it?" Concessa asked, grabbing hold of her husband's arm.

"I've just heard that London has finally received an answer from Rome."

"And?"

"And the emperor states that although he's sorry to hear of our plight, he has no troops to spare. The Visigoths have invaded Italy, and they are now at the walls of Rome."

"Besieging Rome?" Patrick cried in disbelief. "I never thought such a thing was possible! Rome has always seemed so enduring.

If Rome falls, it *will* be the end of the world."

"I agree," Calpornius said sadly, motioning for one of the servants to bring him a drink. "Honorius said that we British will have to defend ourselves from now on. In fact, he said that we'll have to manage all of our own affairs from here on out."

"You mean we're no longer part of the Roman Empire?" Concessa asked.

"That's essentially it. Britain is an independent nation again, through no wish of our own."

The news that Calpornius brought home from time to time continued to get worse. One evening, visibly shaken, he called his entire household together. "I've just received news that Rome has fallen to the Visigoths. They've sacked the entire city."

Several of the household servants began crying when they heard the news. "So Rome is no more?" one servant asked incredulously.

"No, thankfully it's still there," Calpornius sighed. "These Visigoths profess to be Christians, although they have a different understanding of Christ's deity than we do. So in their 'mercy,' they merely *plundered* Rome, rather than destroying it. After several days of robbing and looting, they gave the city back to the emperor."

"Thank God!" Concessa burst out in relief.

"Yes, that's one thing we can be thankful for," Calpornius continued. "But I'm afraid there is little other good news. London reports that authority and structure are breaking down all over Britain. Our whole nation is fragmenting into tribal units, much like the structure before the Romans came."

"What do you mean?" one of the servants asked.

"Well, if a man successfully battles the barbarian invaders in his area—whoever those invaders might be—he elevates himself into a petty king, ruling a small territory. Some of these new 'kings' pretentiously call themselves by Roman titles, such as *dux*. But they have no connection with the government in Rome."

"It sounds like Ireland all over again," Patrick observed.

"Speaking of Ireland, I haven't heard anything from the presbyters in awhile. I think I'll talk to them tomorrow."

"Patrick, how can you think of Ireland at a time like this?" Concessa exclaimed, glaring at her son. "With the world coming to an end, we need you right here."

"If the world is coming to an end," Patrick replied determinedly, "the Irish need to hear the Gospel first."

The next day Patrick visited the presbyters. "I can't believe you're talking about Ireland when our whole nation is about to crumble!" Petronius began, echoing the words of Patrick's mother. "We're struggling just to *preserve* the church. As civilization crumbles around us, about the only thing that gives the British any sense of unity is Christianity. Yet, in these cataclysmic times, many of the peasants are turning back to their old Celtic or Roman gods. There's no point in talking about taking the Gospel to Ireland, when the people need it more right here in Britain."

"Besides that," another presbyter added, "we're also having to fight heresy in our own midst."

"What heresy?" Patrick asked with inquisitive eyes.

"The heresy of Pelagius. You've heard of him haven't you?"

Patrick sat with a blank expression on his face. "No, I'm afraid I haven't," he sheepishly admitted.

"No, I suppose not," another presbyter interjected. "You don't seem to grasp anything theological!" Patrick looked up at the speaker. His name was Longinus Publius Quintus, a highbrow, well-schooled Roman. Quintus was only a few years older than Patrick, and he had only been a presbyter for about a year. Yet, he acted like he was the bishop.

"Well," Quintus explained condescendingly, "Pelagius is a British presbyter who teaches—or at least is accused of teaching—that humans can be saved without God's grace. His teachings have caused great controversy throughout the entire church. It's caused considerable embarrassment to the British church."

"I'm sorry, Patrick," Petronius stated, shaking his head, "but at the moment, the church has much higher priorities than some idealistic scheme to save the pagan Irish."

So the years slowly rolled by, and still Patrick remained in Britain, waiting on God. He continued to live with his parents, helping them as he was able. They kept hoping he would forget about the whole matter of Ireland.

"I spoke with Sextus today," Calpornius remarked to Patrick one day. "You know, his daughter Juliana has come of age. She would make a godly wife, Patrick."

"A wife? How can I possibly think of a wife?" Patrick responded in disbelief. "I could never think of taking a wife to Ireland. It's much too dangerous."

"So it's Ireland again?" Concessa snapped, tossing aside a dress she was mending. "Can't you ever get Ireland out of your head?"

"No, mother, I can't get Ireland out of my head," Patrick stood his ground. "I know beyond any doubt that God has called me there."

"Marcus, Marcus!" Patrick called to his friend one morning. "Do you know what today is?"

Marcus thought for a moment. "No, I guess I don't."

"Today marks six years since God summoned me to Ireland in a dream. You remarked once that God might make me wait six years to return to Ireland, just as he made me wait six years before allowing me to return to Britain."

"Yes, I think I remember saying that," Marcus replied, scratching his head.

"Well, anyway, the presbyters want to speak to me this morning. They didn't say what it was about, but I'm convinced they're going to tell me that they're ready to send me to Ireland. I'm on my way there right now."

Patrick sat down before the presbyters in eager anticipation. "Patrick," Petronius began, "it's been about six years since you began your studies for the ministry. At times your progress has been slow." Patrick's heart began to sink. "Nevertheless, you'll be happy to know that the other presbyters and I have decided to recommend you to the bishop to be ordained as a presbyter."

Patrick's whole face lit up. "Thank you, thank you," he responded as he embraced each of the leaders. "I'll commit myself to honorably carry out my office," he said resolutely. "Does this mean I can go to Ireland now? "

"No," Quintus spoke up. "We don't feel you're ready yet for such an important assignment. First, we would like for you to acquire some experience as a presbyter." Patrick's face fell.

"However, this does mean," Petronius added, "that you are now authorized to preach here in Britain and to celebrate communion." Patrick smiled weakly, holding back tears.

A week after his ordination, Patrick preached his first sermon. "Do you know why we're beset by barbarians on every side?" he challenged the congregation. "Do you know why thousands of us have been taken to Ireland as slaves? God has abandoned *us* because we have abandoned *Him*. We put no trust in Him whatsoever. Instead, we trust our swords and the legions of Rome. Why is nobody *converting* the barbarians? If we brought the love of Christ to them, they wouldn't be attacking us in their hateful fury." A murmur went through the congregation. Some of the people shook their heads and others rolled their eyes.

Undaunted, Patrick continued on, "But most of you are saying that it would be too dangerous to go among the barbarians and try to convert them. You doubt the power of Christ to change hearts as dark as those of the Irish and the Picts. What's more, most of you totally ignore the teachings of Jesus. You ridicule His ministers. You're more concerned about your houses, your wealth, and your personal safety than you are about your *souls*. Do we learn nothing from the lessons of ancient Israel? When did calamities befall them? Wasn't it when they turned their backs on God? Wasn't it when they ignored His commandments? Wasn't it when they worshiped idols either openly or in secret?

Patrick paused to let the import of his words sink in. "Yes, I know that many of you still worship the pagan gods of our ancestors. You profess to be Christians, but at night, you go into the oak groves and worship Brigid and Lugh. What does Christ share with Lugh? You can't sit at the table of the Lord and the table of the demons!"

When communion was over, many of the people left in a huff. "He's nothing but a self-righteous trouble-maker," one of the men grumbled as he walked out.

The years passed by, and Patrick remained in Britain. Meanwhile, presbyters and bishops came and went, and most of them forgot all about Patrick's mission. Victoricus had died. So had Petronius, Patrick's most sympathetic supporter among the leaders. The self-important Quintus was now the main spokesman for the presbyters. Nevertheless, Patrick continued to preach fiery sermons, although few parishioners paid any attention to him. He also continued to beg the British bishops and presbyters to send him to Ireland. But they continually put him off.

"How long, oh Lord?" Patrick cried out daily to God. However, God never told him how long he would have to wait. Nor did God give him permission to embark on his mission alone, without the authority of the church. Although deeply discouraged, Patrick persevered in prayer.

"With each passing year, my love for the Irish grows only stronger," Patrick told Marcus one day.

"You never cease to amaze me, Patrick," Marcus confessed. "I'm afraid I would have given up hope long ago. You must be another Moses. You know, God made Moses wait forty years before sending him back to Egypt."

"Oh no! Surely God won't make me wait forty years. I'm not *that* strong."

"No, surely not," Marcus agreed.[1]

---

[1] *Confessio* §1, 11, 27, 46.

Eleven

A People from Hell

Year after year, Patrick kept praying, and he kept imploring his seniors in the church. But the only answer he ever received was to keep waiting. The years kept slipping by. His parents were now white-haired, and his father walked with the help of a carved oak walking stick. Patrick's own hair was turning gray. The people of Bannavem Taburniae could scarcely believe that this peculiar man was *still* talking about going to Ireland.

Of course, Patrick's mission in life was the least of their worries. They had enough to worry about with the crumbling of Roman Britain.

"Britain used to be one of the most prosperous and well-governed provinces of the Roman Empire," Calpornius commented one evening during supper. "But what is it now? Nothing but a motley collection of walled city-states, petty kingdoms, and vast stretches of no-man's lands ruled by bands of robbers and brigands. More and more peasants are fleeing to the walled cities for protection."

"But you can't blame them for that," Patrick interrupted.

"No, of course not. I would do the same if I were in their shoes. But, as a result, we're now dealing with the new problem of overcrowding. And devastating plagues are running rampant through our crowded cities."

"These things are terrible all right," Patrick said calmly. "But I think the biggest problem our nation is facing right now is its lack of faith. Most of our people profess to be Christians, but very

87

few of them trust in God anymore. They certainly aren't turning to God in this hour of crisis."

Calpornius was quiet for a moment. "I'm afraid your mother and I don't see things the way you do, Patrick," he finally responded, glancing at his wife for support. "We respect you for your faith, but I'm afraid that most of us are looking for some more practical solution than simply praying. In fact, this week the leaders of the various city-states and petty kingdoms are meeting together in council in London to try to find a solution. I'm too old to attend such meetings anymore, but I should be hearing next week what solution, if any, they come up with."

The following week Calpornius received a full report on the council, and one evening he sat down with his entire household and told them what he had learned. "It seems that a new leader emerged from the council. A man named Vortigern."

"Who's he?" Patrick asked.

"I had never heard of him myself. But I've learned that he is one of the petty kings who has enjoyed a measure of success in fighting the Scots. He made a dramatic speech before the council, reminding them that our enemies grow stronger year after year, and we grow weaker. 'We've demonstrated that we can battle the barbarians and win,' he told them. 'But for how long?' He said he had a better plan."

"What was this better plan?" Concessa asked anxiously, leaning forward.

"Well, Vortigern asked the councilmen, 'Who among the invaders are the strongest and most feared?'"

"That would be the Saxons, from what I've heard," Patrick interjected.

"Exactly," Calpornius continued. "The whole assembly acknowledged that. The Saxons must come from hell itself. At least the Irish, Scots, and Picts take captives. But the Saxons slaughter everyone without mercy."

"But what do the Saxons have to do with Vortigern's plans?" Concessa asked with a puzzled expression.

"Well, there's an old saying that the best way to fight fire is with fire. Vortigern argued that the only way to permanently keep the Scots and Picts out of our country is to pit against them a race of men who are even more cruel and evil than they are."

"Don't tell me Vortigern wants to make a deal with the Saxons?" Patrick asked in disbelief.

"Maybe his plan isn't so absurd," Calpornius countered. "Vortigern suggested that we invite the Saxons to settle in northern Britain. That is, in the countryside that has largely been abandoned because of the ravages of the Picts and the Scots. He says we should offer the Saxons free land to farm. That way, they will no longer have to live off of piracy. Instead, they will have enough good farm land to support their families. The only condition that we'll attach to this offer is that they leave us alone and protect us from our enemies."

"You mean invite savage barbarians to settle in our lands?" Concessa asked with a note of alarm. "Does that really make sense?"

"Maybe it doesn't," Calpornius confessed, shrugging his shoulders. "But what Vortigern is suggesting is nothing new. For a hundred years now, the Roman emperors have permitted different Germanic tribes to settle in Gaul and other parts of the empire. Those tribes have quickly become civilized and have provided a buffer zone, protecting the frontiers of the empire from other Germanic peoples. In fact, right now, these former barbarians make up a sizeable portion of the Roman armies."

"What did the council have to say about Vortigern's plan?" Patrick inquired.

"Many of the men were skeptical. But in the end, the assembly agreed to his plan. So they've sent a Saxon-speaking delegation to the Jutland peninsula."

"Where's that?" one of the servants asked as he cleaned the dining table.

"It's along the eastern coast of the North Sea, in the northern part of Europe," Calpornius explained. "Once the delegates arrive there, they will speak to the two primary Saxon chieftains, Hengest and Horsa, and lay out Vortigern's plan to them. So all we can do now is to hope and pray."

"Yes, I'll definitely pray about this matter," Patrick responded as he went off to bed.

A few weeks later, the men at the local barbershop could talk about nothing else than the arrival of the Saxons. Patrick quietly listened while the men discussed the matter. "I hear that a whole fleet of long ships have arrived, carrying thousands of them," one man remarked.

"What do they look like?" another man asked. "I hear they've come straight from hell, with fiery coals instead of eyes and a mass of twisted snakes instead of hair."

"That's silly," Teilo the barber interjected. "The Saxons are handsome, fair-skinned people. They've brought with them their wives and children, their household goods, and their farming implements."

"I bet they also brought with them their swords, their battle axes, and their pagan religion," Patrick added skeptically.

"Oh, don't pay any attention to Patrick," Teilo replied as he finished trimming Patrick's hair. "He's got his head up in the clouds. He criticizes us for bringing in the Saxons, but he wants to go and live with the Irish." All the men laughed.

"But how do we know the Scots and Picts won't drive the Saxons away?" one of the men asked.

"Well, from what I've heard, our delegates specifically talked to the Saxons about the Picts and Scots. And the Saxon chieftains assured our delegates that they don't fear the Scots and Picts in the least," Teilo answered.

"But are they willing to live with us in peace?" another man chimed in.

"Yes," Teilo replied. "Our delegates asked them if they were willing to become farmers instead of raiders. The Saxons assured the delegates that such a thing had always been their desire. The only reason they raid and plunder is that there's no longer enough land in their ancestral homeland for them to farm. So they have turned to raiding out of necessity. But they would far rather farm than to raid other peoples."

"So we're putting our trust in an alliance with people who don't even know God," Patrick interjected, wiping hair off of his clothes. "If my memory serves me correctly, that's exactly why God punished the Israelites. They put their trust in foreign alliances instead of in Him."

"Look, I'm finished with your hair," Teilo retorted, cleaning off the barber's chair. "So you'd best be on your way."

Patrick left the barber shop and rambled back home. His primary concern was neither the Saxons nor the state of Britain. His heart and mind were still in Ireland. He thought of the hundreds of people who were dying every day over there, never having had an opportunity to hear of Christ. He continued to pray to God; he continued to implore the other church leaders. Still, the answer was the same: "Not yet, Patrick. Not yet."[1]

---

[1] Bede *Ecclesiastical History of the English People* §15.

Twelve

Treachery

Twenty years had passed since God had called Patrick back to Ireland, but still the church wouldn't authorize him to go—even though he had now been a presbyter for fourteen years. He continued to preach God's truths without compromise, regardless of the fact that most of the congregation turned deaf ears.

Nevertheless, over a period of time, his forceful preaching attracted a small group of younger men to his side. They were zealous for God and impatient with the spiritually lethargic church of their day. The leader of this group of younger men was a twenty-two year old deacon named Lomman. Born Paulinus Secundus Lommanus, he was a well-educated man. Yet he was also a humble, prayerful man. Patrick had mentored him and his friend Crispus from the time they were boys. One day Lomman told Patrick, "Crispus and I have decided we're going to go to Ireland with you. Perhaps that's where the fields are ripe. The spiritual fields are well past bloom here and are dying."

"Don't give up so easily on the British church," Patrick quickly responded, running his fingers through his gray-blond hair. "God may yet bring it back to life. Besides, who knows when I'll be leaving for Ireland. You'll probably both be married with families by then."

"No, we've both made a commitment never to marry, just like you, Patrick," Lomman replied in a serious tone. "We'll wait to go to Ireland with you, no matter how long it takes. In the meantime, could you begin teaching us Gaelic so that we can witness to the

Irish once we get there?" Patrick didn't take their commitment to accompany him to Ireland very seriously, but he nevertheless agreed to help them learn Gaelic.

Later, he and his friend Marcus were sharing a meal together. "You know, I've been thinking, Patrick," Marcus began. "You've been a presbyter now for fourteen years. I think you deserve to be made a bishop."

Patrick dropped his spoon and roared with laughter. "Marcus, you're indeed my best friend. But me, a bishop? Are you kidding?"

"No, I'm quite serious."

"You can't be," Patrick protested. "I'm hardly worthy of such an honor. Besides, I'm much too rustic and unlearned. I can't even persuade the leaders to send me to Ireland. They would never make me a bishop."

"Well, you never know. God works in mysterious ways," Marcus countered, as he helped himself to an apple.

"To be perfectly honest, the thought of being a bishop has never even entered my mind," Patrick explained. "I simply want to preach the Gospel to the Irish. I'm called to be an evangelist, not a bishop."

"Yes, but if you were a bishop, it would facilitate your setting up churches in Ireland. You well know that all ordinations must be performed by a bishop."

"I see what you mean," Patrick contemplated. "Well, that's in God's hands; I'm not going to worry about it."

The next morning, Patrick noticed a family loading their household goods into a wagon. Hurrying over to them, he saw that it was Gaius, one of the men who still attended church. "You're not leaving us, Gaius, are you?" Patrick asked in disbelief. "You and your parents have lived in Bannavem all of your lives."

"Things are just too dangerous in Britain right now," Gaius replied, shaking his head. "But I'm not the only one leaving. Hundreds of families are fleeing Britain."

"But where will you go?" Patrick asked, as he helped Gaius tie one of the ropes that secured the family's belongings.

"People are going to different places. But a lot of us are moving to Armorica.[1]

"Armorica? Yes, I've heard of it, but I don't know anything about it."

"It's a rocky peninsula off of the southwest coast of Gaul. They say it's the safest place in the whole world right now. It's surrounded by water on the north, west, and south." Gaius drew a rough diagram of Armorica in the air as he talked. "Yet its jagged, rock-strewn coast is sufficiently perilous to deter sea-borne raiders. Dense forests of oak and beech to the east protect it from the mainland barbarians."

"Well, it certainly sounds safe enough," Patrick agreed. "But who will look after your spiritual needs there? Are there any churches?"

"I don't know," Gaius responded, shrugging his shoulders. "If there aren't churches now, I'm sure in time there will be."

"Let me talk to the bishop," Patrick volunteered. "Perhaps he will authorize me to accompany you and the other families to help you get a church started. It would do me good to get away from here for awhile. Besides, I have some dear Christian friends in Gaul that I haven't seen in many years. Perhaps I could travel to Gaul from Armorica and be able to see them."

The next day, Patrick spoke with the bishop, a godly man named Brannoc. "Patrick, I have no objection whatsoever to your going to Armorica with the settlers," Brannoc answered. "They will sorely need your spiritual guidance. I just don't know that this is a good time for you to be gone from the country."

"Why not?" Patrick asked, rather puzzled. "I'm not aware of any pressing responsibilities here."

"Well–uh–I didn't want to say anything, but I guess you'd better know," the bishop stammered. "I've asked the presbyters to select a man to be ordained as an additional bishop. I'm simply too

---

[1] Modern day Brittany, on the southwest coast of France.

old to travel as I once did. In this time of crisis, our people need as much shepherding as possible."

"All right. But what does that have to do with me?"

"Well, your name has been mentioned as a possible candidate for the position."

"Me? A bishop?" Patrick asked in disbelief.

"You certainly have the spiritual qualifications, Patrick. There are other presbyters who are more learned than you—and know their theology better. But there's probably not a presbyter in all of Britain who has your faith. Nor is there anyone who prays the way you do. I would be glad to ordain you as a bishop, if the presbyters select you."

"I guess that's in God's hands," Patrick replied. "What difference will it make whether I'm in Armorica or not?"

"Your name is not the only one that's been mentioned. I'm sure the presbyters will want to meet with each candidate to examine and question them further. If you're out of the country, they may simply pass you by."

"I see what you mean," Patrick pondered as he stroked his gray beard. "Let me do some thinking and praying about this."

That evening, Patrick conferred with Marcus. "You're not going to believe this, Marcus, but bishop Brannoc has told me that the presbyters are considering me as a candidate for the new bishop. You were right after all. I never would have believed it."

"Well, you don't look all that excited about it," Marcus observed. "Why the serious face?"

"Oh, I am excited. But I had planned to accompany the refugees to Armorica to shepherd them there until a permanent presbyter is ordained for them. But that would take me away for a couple of months. The bishop told me he thought it would be unwise for me to leave the country right now."

"Oh, I see what you mean," Marcus said, scratching his head. "But I'm not so sure it would make any difference if you're in Armorica. What better testimony could you give the other presbyters than to be busy at the Lord's work? If you feel that God wants you to shepherd the settlers, then that's what you should do. Besides, I'll be here to speak on your behalf. We're almost like blood brothers. I'm sure I'll be able to answer whatever questions they have. In fact, I can probably speak better on your behalf than you can. Knowing you, you'd sell yourself short."

"What an incredible friend you are, Marcus," Patrick exclaimed, putting his arm around his friend. The two men prayed, then Patrick left Marcus' place to begin preparing for his trip.

Three days later, Patrick boarded a ship loaded with British refugees headed for Armorica. As he strolled on the deck, enjoying the cool ocean air, he realized how refreshing it was to get away from the discouragement and gloom that had enveloped Britain. The ship tacked its way across the channel until the wild rocky coast of Brittany was in sight. With superb seamanship, the experienced captain safely guided the ship into a small inlet on the Armorican coast.

Leaving the ship, Patrick accompanied Gaius and the other voyagers to the settlement. He liked this gently undulating land, cooled by the salty breezes of the sea. Here the settlers could live in peace, supporting themselves from the sea and raising sheep and other animals on the land. Perhaps their hearts would turn once again to God.

"This is indeed a wonderful place, Gaius," Patrick said aloud, as his eyes studied the land around him. "If God hadn't called me to Ireland, I would think of settling here with you."

"So it's still Ireland, is it?" Gaius asked, rather surprised. "I thought you had given up on that idea long ago."

"If it had been *my* idea, I would have. But it's God who has called me there."

Patrick spent a couple of months with the settlers, until a permanent presbyter came from Britain to take his place. After that, Patrick journeyed on to Gaul for a few weeks. He savored his time there with the Christians he had met as a young man on his way back from Ireland.

"I can't tell you how much I've enjoyed my time with you," he finally told his friends. "But I mustn't stay any longer. I need to find out what's happening at home." The next day he departed for Britain.

When Patrick arrived at home, his father met him with a downcast face. "Sit down, Patrick" he said. "I'm afraid I have some discouraging news for you."

"Is it mother?" Patrick asked anxiously, studying his father's face.

"No, your mother is fine. The news is concerning *you*. While you were in Gaul, your name was proposed for ordination as a bishop."

"Yes, I knew that this might happen," Patrick responded with a sigh of relief. "Bishop Brannoc had told me. But Marcus was here to speak up for me."

Calpornius paused for a moment, hesitating to go further. Patrick reassured him, "Father, it isn't going to break my heart if they turned me down as a bishop. I had never asked to be made one in the first place."

"Yes, they turned you down," Calpornius replied soberly, searching for the right words. "But there's more to the story than that. Marcus did speak to the council of presbyters, as you said. However, he–uh–well, he spoke *against* you. Not *for* you."

Patrick could hardly believe what he was hearing. "No, Father, there must be some mistake!" he gasped. "Marcus is the dearest friend I have. He would never say even one word against me."

"Oh, but he did. Worse than that, he brought up something that *I* didn't even know about. He said that you confessed to him that when you were a fifteen you...."

Patrick's face flushed with embarrassment. "He told the presbyters *that*? That happened almost thirty years ago! I scarcely believed in God at the time. What bearing does that have on my ordination now?"

"Apparently, the leaders felt you weren't 'beyond reproach,' one of the qualifications for a bishop. So they nominated Julius instead."

"Julius?" Patrick repeated. He stood up and paced for a few minutes, beginning to calm down. "I guess Julius will make a suitable bishop. I can live with that." He then slumped back down on the couch.

When he sensed that Patrick could handle more, Calpornius continued, "There's still more, son. The story has spread throughout the village. Now everyone knows about it."

Patrick fell on his face, buried his head in his hands and began to sob. "I can't *believe* he would do such a thing! I can't believe it. Why would he betray me like this?"

Calpornius lovingly patted his son's back. They both were silent for a few moments. Finally, Calpornius said softly, "Son, this is the most treacherous thing I've ever heard of. You're a very outspoken person, Patrick, and you've made a lot of enemies over the years. But I never expected that it would be Marcus who would betray you like this."

Sitting up, Patrick squeezed his father's hand reassuringly.

His father continued, "You know that your mother and I have never wanted you to go to Ireland. Yet we're both truly sorry for what has happened. Your name has been blackened unfairly. What's worse—for you, anyway, not for your mother and me—is that I'm quite certain that now they will never authorize you to go to Ireland."[1]

---

[1] *Confessio* §26, 27, 32.

Thirteen

Another Dream

Patrick spent the rest of that day in his room, in prayer. For the first time in years, he began to lose faith in God. However, that night, God once more appeared to him in a dream. In this dream, a group of presbyters and bishops were holding up a written document that condemned Patrick. Suddenly, in the dream, God spoke from heaven to Patrick: "We have seen the face of Marcus with displeasure."[1]

When Patrick awoke the next morning, a ray of hope touched his heart. "Father! Mother!" he shouted as he ran down the stairs. "Let me tell you about my dream."

"Another dream, Patrick?" Calpornius asked, as he hastily finished dressing. Concessa quickly joined her husband, eager to hear about Patrick's new dream.

With a beaming face, Patrick related the events of his dream. "What really excites me is that God didn't say, *'You* have seen Marcus' face with displeasure.' No, He said *'We* have seen his face with displeasure.' In other words, God was including Himself in the situation, as though He were standing by my side through the whole thing."

"Yes," Concessa reflected thoughtfully, "I see what you mean."

"I can't help thinking about the verse that says, 'He who

---

[1] *Confessio* §29.

touches you, touches the apple of my eye,"[1] Patrick noted. Lifting his arms in praise, he continued, "What does it matter that my best friend has betrayed me? What does it matter if the church leaders are against me? God is clearly on my side. That's all that matters."

"What a sudden turn-around of events," Calpornius responded with a big smile. "But what do you think God is going to do *now*?"

"I have no idea," Patrick replied, shrugging his shoulders. "All I know is that if God is for me, who can be against me?"

The family enjoyed a leisurely breakfast together. "You know," Patrick observed between mouthfuls, "Jesus has helped me to understand what He felt when He was betrayed by one of His own apostles. In His mercy, He's let me personally taste a small bit of the anguish He experienced hundreds of years ago. Actually, I've gotten off rather lightly. I've only been crucified with *words*. Jesus was crucified with *nails*." Patrick paused for a moment, taking some more bites and reflecting again on the dream.

But it was quite different news that the people in the village were rejoicing about that morning. "Have you heard the report?" someone excitedly asked Patrick in the street later that morning.

"What report?" Patrick replied with a puzzled look on his face.

"Why, the report about the Saxons! They've already engaged the Picts in battle and have sent them scurrying back to the mountains of the far north. We're finally going to have peace and security again in Britain!"

Patrick thanked the man for the news, and he relayed it to his parents that evening.

"Yes, I heard the same thing from the other decurions this afternoon," Calpornius responded. "Let's just hope the peace lasts. With peace, perhaps we can address the serious economic needs of our country. I don't want to alarm you, but the news I heard concerning our economy is distressing. Our whole Roman way of life is grinding to a slow halt, both economically and govern-

---

[1]Zech. 2:8.

mentally."

"Why, what's happened?" Patrick asked in a concerned voice.

"Well, for one thing, it's been years since any new coinage has been minted. As a result, the whole country is running out of coins. Out of necessity, most people are now bartering for goods and services."

"Well, I'm no stranger to that," Patrick smiled. "I lived with that for years in Ireland."

"Ireland. Yes, before long perhaps Britain will be reduced to the level of Ireland. We once had a thriving economy. Now that's totally collapsed. No taxes have been collected for years. Once, there were good roads connecting all the major cities of Britain. But those roads haven't been maintained in decades, and now they're too dangerous to travel at night. Patrick, I ... Patrick, aren't you listening?"

"I'm sorry father," Patrick quickly apologized, as if coming out of a daydream. "I know I should be all concerned about those things. But I'm afraid that right now my mind is on the lost souls in Ireland. It's been over twenty years since God called me to 'walk again' among the Irish. Now my beard is gray. Yet, here I am—still stuck in Britain."

"Why don't you focus then on the lost souls *here*?" Concessa inquired, gently taking hold of Patrick's hand.

"Oh, I'm definitely concerned about them, too. But nobody pays any attention to my preaching here. I'm afraid Marcus has permanently tarnished my reputation. Not that very many people ever listened to my preaching, anyway. But now, *nobody* does—except Lomman and his group of young men. Everyone else thinks I'm nothing but a self-righteous hypocrite."

Patrick found solace in the company of Lomman, Crispus, and other spiritually minded younger men. Lomman and Crispus had remained true to their word. They never married, but instead had remained steadfast in their commitment to go with Patrick to Ireland. Through Patrick's help, they had even become fluent in Gaelic. Often they accompanied Patrick when he witnessed to

Irish merchants and seamen.

"Have you found it in your heart to forgive Marcus yet?" Lomman asked Patrick one day as they were walking through a nearby meadow.

"Not yet," Patrick answered slowly. "I know I need to. I can't ask Christ to forgive my sins if I don't forgive those of my fellow man. But it's really difficult. I haven't even figured out *why* he did what he did."

"Jealousy, no doubt," Lomman replied.

"Jealousy? Why would *anyone*–let alone Marcus–be jealous of *me*? What do I have that he doesn't?"

"You're a presbyter, and he isn't."

"But Marcus never gave the slightest hint that it bothered him." Patrick sat down on a boulder and removed a pebble from his sandal. "In fact, he was the first one to suggest that I be made a bishop."

"Yes. But maybe his suggestion wasn't sincere," Lomman interjected.

"Obviously it wasn't" Patrick agreed. "Please pray for me. I know I need to forgive him, but I'm really struggling. Anyway, I don't even know where he is. You know, he left town shortly before I returned from Armorica."

"I guess he couldn't bear to face you after what he did," Lomman observed, feeling fiercely loyal toward Patrick. "I hear he lives up the coast now with an uncle."

Four more years passed by tediously. They seemed like an eternity to Patrick. He called out to God, weeping bitter tears, begging Him to give him permission to bypass the church leaders. But God wouldn't allow him. He continued to implore the other leaders, but they paid no heed to his entreaties.

His primary opponent among the clergy continued to be Quintus, who still looked down on Patrick because of his lack of schooling and his poor grasp of theological intricacies. However, later that year, news arrived that made even Quintus reconsider things.

"Father and Mother!" Patrick burst through the front door, leaving it half-opened. "Guess what?" he said, gasping to catch his breath. "I've just learned that the bishop of Rome has sent a man named Paladius to Ireland."

"So Rome is going to try to convert the Irish," Concessa commented, sitting down. "But why are you so excited? Doesn't that mean the door is closed to you now?

"No, I don't think so," Patrick reflected. "As I understand it, Paladius' mission is not so much to convert the pagan Irish as it is to minister to the many Christians who are now in Ireland."

"I didn't realize there were Christians in Ireland," Calpornius responded in surprise.

"Of course there are," Patrick explained. "Think of all of the Christians from Britain who've been taken to Ireland. In addition, some of the Irish have converted to Christianity. As you know, I've converted a few myself from preaching to the Irish merchants in London. Others have been converted through the testimony of their slaves or from contacts with Christians in the course of trade."

"I see," Calpornius said, leaning back in his chair.

"The important thing," Patrick continued, "is that if Rome thinks Ireland is worthy of its attention, how can the British church continue to ignore it?"

Patrick was right. Suddenly, Patrick's request to go to Ireland didn't seem so foolish to his peers. In fact, within a few months, the aged bishop Brannoc called the clergymen of his area into council. "Brothers, we have made a big mistake. In fact, I don't hesitate to say we've sinned against God."

"What are you referring to?" Quintus asked politely.

"Nearly twenty-five years ago, God called a man from our community to go and bring the good news of Christ to the Irish. But today the Irish are still dying without ever having heard of Christ. Why? Because of our lack of faith! We've never sent the man that God chose. Now, Rome has sent a bishop to Ireland. I see this as a direct rebuke from God to the church of Britain. We've failed in our duty. Perhaps now He's by-passed us."

"But it's not too late to send Patrick. Why don't we send him now?" one of the presbyters volunteered. Feeling sheepish, the other leaders hastily agreed.

"So you're ready to have him ordained as a bishop, then?" Brannoc asked.

"Well, no, we don't mean that he would be ordained as a bishop," Quintus explained. "But I think we're all ready to send him as a presbyter."

"I see," Brannoc retorted, "so when he plants churches, he has to take his Irish converts to Rome's bishop so that Rome can ordain them to the ministry. Is that what we want? We plant churches in Ireland just so they can come under Rome's jurisdiction?"

"But what about Patrick's great sin?" another presbyter interjected.

"You mean what he did when he was fifteen? Before he ever knew God?" Brannoc's thin face was flushed with anger. "Patrick's forty-eight years old now. Can he never be forgiven? Do you want to know about the sins I committed before I knew God?"

"But Patrick is so uncouth," Quintus protested. "His Latin is barbaric. After all these years, he still doesn't know the fine points of theology."

"But he knows the Scriptures. Probably better than you do. And more importantly, he knows *God*! That's what matters." Brannoc was visibly flushed and had begun to raise his voice. "No one's asking you to make him a bishop to serve here in Britain. We're talking about making him a bishop for Ireland!"

At last, the reluctant leaders agreed to have Patrick ordained as a bishop of the Irish. When the news of their decision reached Patrick, he was beside himself with joy. He threw back his head and shouted praises to heaven! After telling the news to his parents, he immediately reported it to Lomman, Crispus, and the other young men of their group.

"I know you've said all along that you want to go with me," he told Lomman and Crispus in a serious tone, "but I want you to know that it's still okay to back out. All I can promise you in Ireland are hunger, cold, suffering, and possibly death. You may never see your loved ones again. I fully expect to die in Ireland—but not before many souls are won to Christ. God would not be sending me unless He knew that the Irish were ready to receive the Gospel. I still welcome your help, but make certain this is really what you want to do."

"Our decision was made years ago," Lomman replied without hesitation. "We've already counted the cost. We'd rather die in God's service in Ireland than to spend our lives here, watching our own nation slowly die." Crispus nodded his head in agreement. Later that week, two of the other young men in their group volunteered to join the mission.

Patrick's parents generously supported Patrick's mission by donating food, clothing, items for barter, and other supplies. Brannoc saw to it that the British church provided some additional supplies. Eventually, the day of Patrick's ordination arrived. It didn't take place in his home village of Bannavem Taburniae, but at Corinium, a larger city not too far away. Three bishops, dozens of presbyters and deacons, and a number of other people were present. Patrick was in tears during most of the service—both tears of joy and tears of sorrow at his own unworthiness. He realized that he had never completely forgiven Marcus. "Please forgive him, Father," Patrick prayed silently. "I forgive him for what he has done." Patrick immediately felt a great weight lifted off of his shoulders.

Finally, the three bishops laid their hands on Patrick and one of them prayed over him. As the bishop prayed, Patrick felt the anointing of the Holy Spirit on his soul. The deacons then brought Patrick the bread and wine, and Patrick celebrated communion with the congregation.

At the conclusion of the ordination, all of the people came up to Patrick in single file to be blessed by him, as was the custom. He warmly greeted each person and laid his hands on them to bless them. Looking up, he suddenly noticed Marcus sitting at the back of the church. Patrick smiled, looking forward to blessing Marcus and giving him the kiss of peace. However, rather than coming up to greet Patrick, Marcus quietly slipped out the door and slowly walked away from the church. Patrick prayed inwardly that Marcus would come back, but he didn't.

A few weeks later, a small crowd assembled on a narrow, sandy beach surrounded by rocks, where Patrick's boat was ready to sail. Patrick addressed the group briefly and then tenderly kissed his aged parents good-bye. With that, he set sail for Ireland.

From a rocky ledge in the distance, a solitary figure watched Patrick leave, gazing at the small boat until it disappeared in the mist. The man then broke down and wept.[1]

---

[1] *Confessio* §26, 29.

Fourteen

Ireland at Last!

"What a strange feeling this is," Patrick said to Lomman as their boat skimmed over the choppy Irish Sea. "I can't help but think about the other time I traveled by boat to Ireland."

"Those have to be pretty unpleasant memories," Lomman responded as he adjusted the sails. "I can't even begin to imagine what a nightmare that day must have been. How old did you say you were at the time?"

"Sixteen."

"Do you think your master is still alive?" Crispus asked.

"I doubt it. He was at least fifty when I escaped from Ireland, and that was twenty-five years ago."

"If his sons hear you're in Ireland, will they come to reclaim you?" Lomman inquired.

"Perhaps. I've been wondering the same thing. All I know is that my life is in God's hands. I firmly believe that He won't allow me to be killed or enslaved until His mission through me is accomplished."

The next day, Patrick and his men landed on a deserted beach on the northeastern coast of Ireland. After thanking God for their safe journey, they set up camp near the shore. They enjoyed a simple meal that evening, sang Psalms together, prayed at length, and finally went to sleep. Arising before dawn the next morning, they prayed for more than an hour, asking for God's guidance as they set out to bring the Gospel to the Irish. After a light breakfast, they began their journey, spotting a sheep trail that served as a road. Soon they met an elderly peasant man carrying a large bundle of sticks on his back.

Speaking in Gaelic, Patrick approached the man, "Greetings! We've come from Britain to bring an important message of good news to the people of Ireland. Can you tell me the name of the king of this *tuatha*?"

"The name of the king is Laoghaire,"[1] the old man replied in a wavering voice.

"And where does he live?" Patrick asked.

Pointing his bony finger down the path, he said, "Just follow this road and you will come to his house soon enough." Patrick thanked the peasant, and he and his band followed the meandering road in the direction the man had indicated. After they had journeyed about a mile, Lomman suddenly exclaimed, "Patrick, look on top of the hill ahead! Armed warriors!" He pointed to three statuesque warriors, spears in hand, who stood watching the small band. "Are we in danger?"

"Of course we're in danger!" Patrick replied. "We're in *serious* danger. But it's absolutely essential that none of us show any sign of fear. Keep your heads up and continue to walk straight ahead with a brisk pace. Lomman, start praying and don't stop no matter what happens ahead. I'll lead the rest of us in singing a Psalm."

In a loud, clear voice, Patrick began singing, "Deliver me from my enemies, O my God...." The others (except for Lomman) soon joined in the familiar words of Psalm 59. Finding their courage in God, the army of spiritual warriors continued their advance, singing and praying as they went. As they rounded a hill, they found their way blocked by the three brawny warriors, who stared at them menacingly.

"Who are you and what do you want?" one of the warriors growled at them.

"We are ambassadors of a great king," Patrick replied without wavering. "We have come across the sea in a mission of peace to

---

[1]Pronounced LEER ee.

bring a message of good news to Laoghaire, your king."

The three warriors hesitated for a few seconds, taken aback both by Patrick's boldness and by the nature of his mission. Finally, one of them bellowed, "Go away! Or else our king will cut off your heads and hang them above his doorway."

"Go tell Laoghaire that we do not fear his threats," Patrick replied firmly, staring the warrior straight in the eyes.

Again the warriors hesitated, not sure of what to make of these strange visitors. Finally, they huddled together. "This could be a trick," one of them posited in a hushed voice.

"Yes, but if they're who they say they are, Laoghaire will have our heads if we turn them away," another replied.

"Let's search them for weapons," the third warrior suggested. "If they're unarmed, we'll take them to Laoghaire. If they're armed, we'll chase them away." The others quickly agreed with this plan.

The warriors briskly searched Patrick and his men, along with their baggage. They, of course, found no weapons—other than utility knives with the food supplies. "Follow me," one of the warriors finally grunted to Patrick, motioning with his arm. So the small band continued up the road, with one of the Irish warriors leading the way and the other two bringing up the rear.

When they finally reached the king's longhouse, one of the warriors told the visitors to remain outside while he spoke to Laoghaire. Patrick and his men waited anxiously, praying silently with great fervor.

"Do you think Laoghaire will receive us?" Lomman asked anxiously. "Or will he kill us and decorate the doorposts with our heads?"

"I can't believe God would finally bring us to Ireland only to have us killed the first day," Patrick replied calmly. "However, as to whether or not this king will hear us—that's in God's hands."

Eventually, the warrior returned and announced that the king would receive them that night at a feast. He then led Patrick and the others to a small hut where they could rest until the evening.

That night, a servant led Patrick and his men inside Laoghaire's longhouse. When he entered the great hall, Patrick cast his observant eyes around the room. In the center stood a long oak table, which was little more than a series of planks of rough-hewn wood from the forest. It rested on supports that raised the planks about a foot off of the floor. Although there was no cloth on the table, it seemed already prepared for the evening meal. There were no benches, chairs, or other seats; animal skins spread around the table would serve for seating.

The room had no ceiling—only the rafters and thatch of the roof. At one end of the room stood a massive fireplace. It had no chimney, leaving the smoke to find its way out through the rafters and thatch. Glancing overhead, Patrick noticed that the beams were encrusted with the black varnish of soot. The floor was nothing more than earth and lime, pounded into a hard substance, covered in some places with animal skins.

Several domestics were scurrying about, making final preparations for the great feast. Soon servants entered the room carrying wooden vessels stacked high with food. And what a feast it was! At one end of the table, wooden platters were heaped with the meat of a freshly killed boar. There were also platters of venison, mutton, and rabbits. Elsewhere on the large table, there were plates of fish, bowls of butter, huge loaves of barley bread, and pots of honey.

As the guest of honor this evening, Patrick sat cross-legged on the floor facing the doorway. King Laoghaire sat to his left. He was a tall, red-faced man, with a huge drooping mustache that trapped the food he was eating. Gray locks of unkempt hair hung down to his shoulders from his balding head. He was dressed in colorful red and blue checkered pants and a bright scarlet tunic that reached down to his upper thighs. The tunic was held around his slim waist with an ox-hide belt, ornately decorated with golden scroll work. A long emerald-green cape covered his back and was held around his neck with a gold brooch. His powerful arms were adorned with golden torques, worn as bracelets. Most of the other men were dressed similarly.

The only eating utensil the men used was an occasional dagger to stab a piece of meat. Otherwise, the people were content to eat with their hands. The master and guest of honor drank from silver goblets. Other guests drank from bronze cups or drinking horns that were passed around from guest to guest.

The women sat at a similarly arranged table, and they ate in the same fashion as the men. Most of them were dressed in long, flowing, brightly-colored dresses, some of which were made of silk. Golden embroidery embellished the hems and necks of many of the dresses. All the women wore their hair in finely twisted braids or elaborate coiffures. They were arrayed with gold or silver torques around their necks and jangling bracelets around their wrists.

At both tables, the guests were engaged in lively discussions, and the room often rang with laughter. As the evening wore on, heated quarrels broke out at both tables. One of the young warriors seemed to be jeering at another warrior seated at the king's table. Suddenly, the two men sprang to their feet and lunged at each other with drawn daggers. Probably one of them would have killed the other if the king had not intervened, entreating both men to sit down.

Laoghaire then stood and announced to his guests, "We have an important visitor with us tonight. He has come to us from across the sea, bringing a message of good news to us from a great king." Motioning to Patrick, the king continued, "Stand and tell us about your mission." He then sat down and gestured to a servant to refill his goblet.

Patrick stood up and surveyed the crowd before him, silently praying to God for the right words to speak. "Your king has spoken correctly," Patrick began in a loud voice. "I have come from across the sea—from Britain. But the king I represent is far greater than any king or governor of Britain. He is more powerful than even the emperor of the Romans."

Patrick paused briefly, letting the import of his words sink in.

The guests had now grown quiet and were listening with eager anticipation. "I have been sent here by a king who not only governs the whole earth—but the entire universe as well. His name is Jesus Christ. He is the Son of God. Yet He once lived on earth as a man, just like you and me. He came to earth to bring us *good news*. Good news for everyone—good news for the Romans, good news for the Britons, good news for the Irish." Patrick paused once again.

"What is this good news?" Laoghaire asked aloud.

"The good news is that the gods you have worshiped and feared are not gods at all. They are merely demons. I'm talking about Teutates, Lugh, Belenos, and the hundreds of other gods that you worship and that my ancestors used to worship. Tell me, how would you describe Belenos? Do you see him as a loving father? Or is he someone you fear?"

"He's no loving father," Fedilmid, one of the king's sons blurted out. "Belenos is lord; he is master. We dare not say anything against him or he will punish us. We must constantly appease him, or he will bring curses down on us."

"What if I told you that this Jesus I speak of can give you power over Belenos? That instead of fearing Belenos, he will fear *you*? What if I told you that the subjects of Jesus have power over *all* your gods? And not just *your* gods—but the ancient gods of the Romans and of all the other nations on earth? What if I told you that the subjects of Jesus no longer have to offer any sacrifices to appease the gods—yet the gods are powerless to punish them?"

"That, indeed, would be good news," Laoghaire agreed.

"But that's not all," Patrick continued. "What if I told you that above all of these so-called gods, there is an Almighty God. He has no name. We, the subjects of Jesus, simply call him Father. We use that name because that's what He is. He loves us more tenderly than even our earthly fathers. In fact, He loves us so much that he gave His only Son to die for us. Your gods demand that you offer human sacrifices to them. But the Almighty God gave His beloved Son as a sacrifice *for us*. His Son, Jesus Christ, died not only for those people who worship Him, but for all man-kind—including the Irish.

"The truth of the matter is that there is no other God–nor has there ever been, nor shall there be hereafter–but this God of whom I speak. That is, the Father, together with His Son, Jesus Christ. The Father is unbegotten and without beginning. His Son Jesus has always existed with Him. Jesus has created all things visible and invisible. Yet, He became man in order to save us and to conquer death. The Father raised His Son from the dead and has given Him a kingdom that will crush and bring an end to all of the kingdoms on earth. Those people who serve Him will eventually become kings and reign with him in the heavens. And He will return some day—perhaps very soon. Even now, He gives us power through the Holy Spirit."

"But what about the sun?" one of the king's attendants asked. "Surely, the sun is god as well."

"No," Patrick responded emphatically. "The sun is *not* god. Rather, it rises each day for us at the command of the Father. The sun will never reign, nor will its splendor last. And those who worship it will never reign either. Instead, they will forfeit eternal life. In contrast, those who believe in and worship the true Sun, Christ, will inherit eternal life. He guards, protects and provides for those who willingly serve Him. His Father adopts all of them as his sons and daughters."

"What you say is wonderful beyond belief," Fedelm, one of the king's daughters, volunteered. "But how do we know it's true?"

"I'm living proof that what I say is true," Patrick responded. "You may be wondering how I've come to speak your language fluently. The reason is that when I was sixteen, I was captured by Irish warriors and sold as a slave here in Ireland to a man named Milchu. I worked as his slave for six years near the Wood of Voclut. But then my God intervened and told me to run away because he had provided a ship for me. I did as my God directed, and I have been a free man ever since."

Some of the guests gasped when they heard that Patrick was a runaway slave. Many of Patrick's listeners began murmuring among themselves, and two of Laoghaire's warriors rose to seize Patrick. However, with a broad gesture from both of his arms, Laoghaire silenced the crowd. His warriors immediately sat back down.

"You are either the most courageous man I have ever met," the king observed, "or else you are an utter fool. Right now, I'm not sure which. I don't know if this Milchu is still living or not. But when he or his sons find out that you're back in Ireland, they will kill you. Of that, I'm certain."

"I have no fear of either Milchu or his sons. I came to Ireland to die. But I know that the King I serve will not let Milchu or anyone else harm me until the work He has sent me to accomplish has been finished. Of that, *I'm* certain." After a dramatic pause, Patrick added, "Let me explain why I'm so certain. I'm certain because the Lord my God showed mercy to me even when I was young and ignorant. He watched over me before I knew him. Before I knew good from evil, He protected me and consoled me as a father would his son."

Patrick went on to describe in detail the dreams he had had while serving Milchu and how God had miraculously directed his escape right to the cove where a boat was waiting. He told the crowd about his second captivity to the ship's crew and how he was delivered from them. He related how his God had supplied food for the starving men, which their gods had been unable to do.

"When I finally got back to my home in Britain, I never wanted to set foot in Ireland again. But my King, Jesus Christ, told me to return here to bring you the good news of His kingdom. You see, it was my God who sent me to Ireland in the first place. He sent me here to learn your language and customs so that later I could return as His messenger to the Irish. And now I cannot keep silent about Him, for He has bestowed so many favors and graces upon me."

Patrick's voice was becoming husky from speaking, and he

asked for a drink of water. He sipped the water slowly, while the assembled guests spoke to one another in hushed tones about the incredible things they were hearing. "God is opening their hearts; He's opening their hearts," Patrick said to himself. "Thank you, Father." He finished his drink and then told the group how Jesus had prophesied hundreds of years before that this good news would reach the Irish.

"As I've stated, He said that He would return to the earth. But He also said that first the good news of His kingdom would be preached in all of the inhabited earth. He told his followers, 'I have set you to be a light for the Gentiles that you may bring salvation to the uttermost ends of the earth.'[1] That is now happening. Ireland is at the end of the earth. Jesus knew in advance that one of his servants would bring this message to you so that you can become adopted children of His Father just as I have."

"I would like to become an adopted son of this Father you speak of," a guest at the table interjected. "How can I do this?"

"It's simple—yet very difficult. It's only for the courageous. Jesus accepts no cowards as His subjects. But the hour is now late. With the permission of your king, I will tell you tomorrow how you—in fact, how all of you—can become adopted children of the Father of the universe."[2]

---

[1] *Confessio* § 38, quoting Isa. 49:6.

[2] *Confessio* §2-4, 38-41, 61; *Epistolo* §5.

Fifteen

The Irish Hear The Gospel

After returning to his room, Patrick stayed up late into the night in prayer, interceding with tears on behalf of the people to whom he had witnessed. Dawn found him and his companions once again on their knees in earnest prayer. After praying, the men read from the Scriptures and sang some of the Psalms together.

After a light breakfast, King Laoghaire, his family, and their guests assembled outdoors in the shade of some large, spreading oak trees. Patrick stood up and addressed the assembly once again: "Last night, I told you that it was both easy and difficult to become an adopted child of the Father. It's simple because Jesus' yoke is easy and light. He is no Belenos who rules by fear. Rather He rules in love. He cares personally for each one of His subjects.

"At the same time, to become a subject of His kingdom, you must be willing to live by the laws of that kingdom. Yet, it's impossible for any natural man or woman anywhere to live by those laws. You can live by them only if you're born a second time. When you're born a second time, you *can* live by those laws through the grace He gives you." Patrick went on to explain what he meant by being born again. He also told his hearers about the laws of Christ from the Sermon on the Mount. After that, everyone enjoyed a meal together and rested for awhile.

"I'm just not sure that I'm getting through," Patrick told the other men uneasily. "I wish I knew some way to present the gospel that would really speak to their culture."

"You mean the way Paul preached to the Athenians on Mars

Hill?" Lomman interjected.

"Exactly. I can't help but reflect on the way that Paul told them, 'As I was passing through and considering the objects of your worship, I even found an altar with this inscription: To the Unknown God. Therefore, the One whom you worship without knowing, Him I proclaim to you.'[1] So Paul presented the gospel in a way to which the Greeks could relate."

"Yes, Paul even added, 'For in Him we live and move and have our being, as also some of your own poets have said, For we are also His offspring.'[2] There, he was actually quoting from their own poet, Menander," Lomman explained.

"I never realized that," Patrick reflected, thinking hard. "Now, if the Greeks had 'seeds of truth' in their culture that Paul could use in presenting the gospel to them, I'm sure the Irish do as well."

"You lived here for six years," Crispus reminded Patrick. "What did you learn about their religion during that time?"

Patrick racked his brain for a few moments. "Well, for one thing, they believe in an immortal soul, just as we do."

"Hallelujah!" Lomman exclaimed. "That will pave the way to teach them what the Scriptures say about life after death and the day of judgment. What other things can you remember?"

"Well, another thing is they believe that pools and springs of water are sacred. Perhaps that's a seed of truth I can use to explain baptism."

"I've heard that they think certain trees are sacred," Crispus added. "Is that correct?"

"Yes, it is. But how will that help us?"

"Well, couldn't you use that as a stepping stone to explain that our first human parents fell because of eating the forbidden fruit of the *tree* of knowledge?"

"Perhaps so," Patrick answered thoughtfully. "That's a good

---

[1]Acts 17:23.

[2]Acts 17:28.

point. In fact, in Paradise, Christians will eat of the *tree* of life.[1] What's more, the Scriptures say that Christ died on a *tree*.[2] This is getting exciting!"

The men finished eating while the Spirit brought more things to Patrick's mind. "God has just reminded me of something else," he told the others excitedly. "The Druids teach that the number three is sacred. They even have a special triad of gods—Taranis, Esus, and Teutates."

"Just like the Trinity," Lomman blurted out.

"Well, sort of. But their triad is very different from our Trinity. Still, it will provide me with a common frame of reference to explain the Trinity."

Everyone had finished eating and relaxing, so Patrick began to teach some more, using some of the points of reference that he and his men had explored. It was late afternoon when Patrick finished. He sat down under a large rowan tree to rest for a moment and survey the crowd before him.

"So what do we have to do to be adopted, to be—what did you call it—born a second time?" one of the king's guests asked.

Although tired, Patrick stood up again, and the Spirit brought to mind the words of Paul to the Philippian jailer. "First of all, you must believe in Jesus Christ with all of your hearts. You must believe that He is the Son of God and that He died for your sins."

Patrick then thought about Peter's answer to the Jews on the day of Pentecost. "Secondly," he added, "You must repent of the way you have been living. Then, you must be converted. That is, you must resolve to leave your past way of life and live from now on for Christ, abiding by His teachings. Finally, you must be baptized in water and in the Holy Spirit for the forgiveness of your sins. In this manner, you are born again and receive adoption as children of God."

---

[1] Rev. 2:7.

[2] Acts 5:30.

Patrick looked with compassion on the anxious faces before him. He sensed that God had opened their hearts to receive the Gospel. In a powerful voice, he asked, "How many of you want to receive this new birth? How many of you want to follow Christ as your king?" Patrick could not hold back the tears as a large number of the people came up and fell on their knees before him. Laoghaire's son Fedilmid and his daughter Fedelm were among those who were ready to be reborn.[1] Patrick lovingly embraced as many of the penitent hearers he could.

Remembering his experience with the sailors, Patrick addressed the assembly once again in a solemn voice. "For twenty-five years, I've waited and prayed for this day. But I need to warn you about something. This is not a step to take lightly. Once you become a Christian, there is no turning back. It would be far better never to become a Christian, than to become one and then revert to your former ways.

"Christ is a king who demands exclusive devotion. Don't imagine that you can become one of His subjects and still worship your other gods also. He won't accept this. Once you are reborn, you can no longer celebrate the festivals of your old gods. There will be no more Beltains or Samains. You can no longer live at war with your neighbors, plunder other nations, or live in drunkenness. And because you won't be doing these things, others will think you're strange. They will even hate you, and they may put some of you to death. If you're not ready to lay down your life for Christ as He laid down His life for you, come no further."

Some of Patrick's hearers slowly backed away, but most of them remained firm. Patrick then knelt and prayed at length for those who were ready to be born again. He directed them to confess their sins before God and to tell God that they wanted to be reborn as His children. After everyone had prayed at length, Patrick then led the group to a nearby lake. At the shore of the lake, he addressed them, "Our king, Christ Jesus, told us this about

---

[1]King Laoghaire himself never embraced Christianity.

His coming: He said that just as the lightning comes from the east and flashes to the west, so likewise His return will be.[1] Christians have always understood this to mean that when Christ returns, He will come from the east. For that reason, we associate the east with the realm of Christ and the west with the realm of Satan.

"Therefore, I want all of you to turn around and face the west. Now, repeat after me, 'I renounce Satan, his angels, and all of his ceremonies and works. I renounce Belenos, Lugh, Taranis, and Brigid.'"

After the group had done that, Patrick continued, "Now, turn back around and face the east. Do you believe in Jesus Christ, the Son of the Living God?"

The group answered in unison that they did.

"Do you accept Him as your Savior and desire to follow Him as your Lord?"

Again, the group answered in the affirmative.

"Do you desire to be baptized in the name of the Father, Son, and the Holy Spirit for the forgiveness of your sins and to become children of God?"

After the group assented, Patrick went on, "With the help of God, will you obediently keep God's holy will and commandments and walk in them all the days of your life?"

When the new believers had answered the last question with a resounding "Yes," Patrick and Lomman waded out into the water, and as the people came forward they baptized them one by one.[2]

When the last person had been baptized, Patrick had the new Christians line up single file. He then invited each of them to come

---

[1]Matt. 24:27.

[2]If this had been back in Britain, an attendant would have handed a white robe to each of the newly baptized Christians to put on. This was an ancient practice of the Church, symbolizing the forgiveness of their sins and their birth as new Christians. However, Patrick had no such robes available at this first baptism in Ireland.

forward and kneel in front of him. As they did so, he laid his hands on them and prayed for them to receive the Holy Spirit. He then took a small flask of scented oil from Lomman, dipped his finger in it, and traced the sign of the cross on the forehead of each person. Soon the air was filled with the heavenly aroma of myrrh.

"I want to explain to you what I'm doing," Patrick told them. "I've traced the figure of the cross on your foreheads to signify that you are now the property of Jesus Christ. You are no longer under the dominion of Belenos or Lugh or Taranis. Over one thousand years ago, a prophet of the Jews foretold that persons would receive this mark on their foreheads. He saw a vision in which a man with a writer's..." Patrick stammered for a few seconds, realizing that there was no word in Gaelic for "ink horn," since they had no written language.

"Uh–that is–a man with a bowl of black paint," he continued. "Anyway, the man in the vision went to all the persons who worshiped the true God and marked what we call the letter T, which is in the form of a cross, on their foreheads." Patrick drew the letter T in the air with his forefinger, to show its shape to the people. "That was a prophetic vision of what we're doing today."[1]

As his newly baptized flock reclined on the grass, Patrick reflected upon the six years he had spent as a shepherd in Ireland. Now once again he was a shepherd. Only this time, the sheep were different. Would he be able to shepherd his new Master's flocks as well as he had shepherded Milchu's flocks?[2]

---

[1]Ezek. 9:4. In the Septuagint, this passage reads, "Put a *tau* [Greek letter "T"] on the foreheads of the men who groan and grieve for all the iniquities that are done."

[2]*Confessio* §14, 38-40; *Epistolo* §3.

Sixteen

A New Kind of Hero

Having lived with the Irish people, Patrick well understood the important role the hero played in their culture. "From what I've heard," he told his men, "in battle, the Irish depend more upon the extreme bravery of one or more of their heroic warriors than they do upon any battle strategy or unified discipline. Often, their hero challenges the enemy to send out their champion to engage him in single combat. At other times, the hero even offers himself as a sacrifice for the good of his people."

"Yes, I've heard that before," Lomman chimed in. "That's one reason the Irish so terrorize our people."

Thinking hard, Patrick continued, "So we've got to give the Irish a new heroic model to replace their warrior-hero ideal. But who will this new hero be?" He paused for a moment. "Why, of course, how silly of me. Their new hero will be Jesus Himself. Jesus forsook all of the comforts of heaven and all of the privileges of Deity in order to come to earth on our behalf. He then single-handedly defeated Satan. I think the Irish can relate to that and respect it."

"You said that the Irish hero often gives up his life as a sacrifice," Crispus interjected. "Jesus also gave His life as a sacrifice for all of mankind."

"Right you are," Patrick replied.

"Of course, in other ways, Jesus doesn't fit the Irish ideal of the hero at all," Patrick mused. "The Irish practically worship beauty. Their kings have to be physically attractive. Yet Jesus wasn't handsome.[1] Furthermore, He didn't come to earth with a sword, slaughtering His enemies. Rather, He came as a suffering servant. He preached love and forgiveness of enemies, not war and hate. These are going to be new things for the Irish. To them, Jesus will be a new kind of hero."

During that first year in Ireland, hundreds of Irish men and women committed their lives to this new hero, Jesus Christ, and received the adoption as sons and daughters of God. Lomman, Crispus, and the others proved to be able assistants. Periodically, Christians from Britain would come over, bringing fresh supplies for the Ireland mission. Although the beleaguered British church couldn't contribute a lot in the way of supplies, Patrick appreciated what help it did provide.

"The important thing," Patrick counseled his men one morning, "is that we must all become living examples of how even fallen humans can live the Christ-life. Like Paul before us, we'll have to browbeat our bodies in order to keep our feet on the narrow way that Christ has set before us. We're on a stage here, and it's important that in our conduct we never give the unbelievers any opportunity to disparage Christ—even in the smallest matter."

"That's going to be extremely difficult," Crispus replied.

"In our own strength, it's impossible," Patrick agreed. "But with the power of the Holy Spirit, we *can* do it. I don't trust my own flesh as long as I'm in this body of death. I know how strong Satan is, and I realize that every day he strives to turn all of us away from the faith. We can only accomplish what we've set out to do if the Lord wills it and guards us from every evil way."

Because they walked closely with the Lord and depended on God's grace, Patrick, his men, and their message had a dramatic effect on their listeners. Everywhere they went, crowds of people laid down their swords forever and committed their lives to Christ. Within a few years, Patrick had baptized thousands of people and

---

[1]Isa. 53:2.

had ordained many of the Irish men into the ministry.

"I've just come back from visiting Bron," Lomman told Patrick one evening, warming himself by the peat fire in their crude, waddle-and-daub hut.

"I wish I could've been with you," Patrick sighed. "That man has given up *everything* for Christ—rank, property, and comforts. Free of the cares of this world, he's been able to devote his life wholeheartedly to Christ."

"Yes, and there are scores of others just like him," Lomman agreed.

"How's he doing?" Patrick inquired.

"He's doing fine, both physically and spiritually. He's built himself a small hut in the mountains of Mourne. There, he spends his entire life in prayer, fasting, and studying Scripture."

"How is he coming with his Latin?"[1]

"He's doing really well. These Irish amaze me. For all of these centuries they've been an illiterate people. Yet now that we're offering to teach them to read, they're embracing it with more zeal than our own people. They *love* to read. Bron is a perfect example of this."

"But is that all he does?" Patrick queried. "He just stays to himself and reads?"

"Not at all. As his reputation for godliness has grown, others have come to him for spiritual counseling and instruction. So now, a number of other single men have constructed huts nearby. And they're the strangest huts I've ever seen. They look like giant beehives. They build them by stacking stones on top of one another, without a drop of mortar."

"Yes, I'm familiar with these 'beehive' huts," Patrick explained as he stoked the fire. "They're actually quite sturdy, and they keep the water out. But tell me more about this community of men. What do they do besides pray, meditate, and study?"

---

[1]Since the Irish had no written language or alphabet, Patrick and his men taught them to read and write in Latin.

"They've become an effective center for evangelism. The men are spreading the gospel all throughout Ulster.[1]

"Praise God!" Patrick exclaimed, raising his hands in the air. "It seems as though He has set this entire nation on fire. And so far, Satan and his demons have been utterly unable to stop it. As you well know, Lomman, it isn't just the men who are eagerly receiving the Gospel. The women are just as eager, or perhaps more so. And they, too, have to make a lot of changes to become Christians."

"How I well know," Lomman agreed. "I think they're as warlike as their men. Just last week, I witnessed an unbelievable fight between two women. One woman had found out that her rival had committed adultery with her husband. So without warning, she fell on the other woman—screaming, kicking, and punching with all of her might. When a bystander tried to break it up, she pummeled him with kicks and punches as well."

Patrick smiled. "Yes, I've witnessed many such fights myself. The women here are also quite loose sexually. Often, they openly commit adultery with their much admired warrior heroes."

"And are they ever preoccupied with beauty and cosmetics!" Lomman interjected. "Have you noticed how they darken their eyebrows with berry juice, paint their fingernails, and even use a special herb to redden their cheeks?"

"How could I help but notice? And, of course, they love to array themselves with costly jewelry and ornate dresses. That's why I so admire our female converts here in Ireland. They give up so much for Christ, becoming fine examples of the godly woman that Peter describes. Hundreds of them have become virgins espoused to Christ. These women are well known throughout their communities for their acts of love, hospitality and mercy."

"In some ways," Lomman added, "I think the celibate life is more difficult for them."

"Why do you say that?" Patrick asked.

---

[1]Northern Ireland.

"Because they usually remain at home, rather than living in community with other virgin women."

"I agree, their lot is difficult. Often their unbelieving parents strongly oppose them. In fact, just last week, Ethne came up to me after we had celebrated the Eucharist."

"Who's Ethne?"

"She's a godly young woman of noble birth. And very beautiful. She could have her pick of dozens of suitors."

"Yes, I remember her now."

"Anyway, she came up and told Crispus and me that she had received a word from a messenger of God. He had admonished her to become a virgin of Christ and to devote her life completely to God.[1] Six days later, she committed herself to be a virgin for Christ. Poor thing, her father was furious and threatened to beat her. In fact, he threatened me as well."

Lomman helped himself to some of the soup cooking in a black iron cauldron hanging over the fire. "Patrick, isn't it about time that you took a rest from your work here and went back to Britain for a short spell? We've been here five years now, and you haven't left the country even once."

"Oh, how I would love to," Patrick sighed with a deep yearning in his eyes. "I can't tell you how much I want to see my family again. And it would be so wonderful to visit some of the brothers in Britain—and maybe even my friends in Gaul. I sometimes feel like I'm in exile here. However, the Spirit won't let me leave Ireland. In fact, He's told me that my work here will be in great peril if ever I leave.[2] So until the Spirit tells me differently, I can't leave."

"Not even for a week?" Lomman asked in disbelief.

"No, not even for a week. I love my parents deeply, and I ache to see them. Yet, my first loyalty must be to my flock in Ireland.

---

[1]*Confessio* §42.

[2]Ibid. §43.

And I have to obey the Spirit. As Jesus said, 'He who loves father or mother more than me is not worthy of me.'" Overcome with emotion, Patrick could speak no more. He went outside and brought in some more firewood.

Lomman helped him put the wood in the fire. He then put his arm around Patrick and said, "I'm going to make it a point to intercede for you on this matter, dear brother. Perhaps God will change His mind and let you leave for at least a week."[1]

---

[1]*Confessio* §41-44, 48; *Epistolo* §12.

Seventeen

The Saxon Fury

Ten years had passed since Patrick had begun his mission in Ireland. However, God had not relented on the matter of Patrick's leaving Ireland. Nevertheless, God did continue to bless Patrick's work. In fact, in the areas where he and his men had heavily evangelized, Christians typically outnumbered the pagans. In those areas, Christianity was dramatically affecting society as a whole. Clans who had been feuding for years laid down their swords and began to love each others as brothers. By this time, Patrick had set up his permanent base at Armagh, in northern Ireland.

"Welcome to Armagh," Patrick said in Latin with outstretched arms to the two guests who approached his simple wattle-and-daub hut one day. "From your dress, I can tell you're not from Ireland."

"No, we're not," the older of the two men replied with a broad smile on his face. "I'm Secundinus and this is Auxilius. We've come to volunteer our services in the work here in Ireland."

Patrick immediately invited the men into his hut and gave them cool water to drink. "Here are our letters of recommendation from bishop Brannoc," Auxilius said as he handed Patrick some papers he had pulled from his worn leather satchel. Patrick studied them for a moment.

"So you're both presbyters, I see. That's wonderful. I can put you to work right away. However, you'll be limited in what you can do here until you learn Gaelic."

"Yes, we realize that," Secundinus responded, nodding his

head. "We're ready to study Gaelic right away."

"Good! I'll ask one of the brothers here to begin teaching you Gaelic this week." Patrick walked over to the lone cupboard in his Spartan hut and produced a loaf of bread and a small bit of cheese from it. "Here, have a bite to eat while you're resting your weary legs."

"During our walk from the coast, Auxilius and I have been remarking on how beautiful Ireland is," Secundinus mentioned between bites. "We come from Gaul originally. Gaul is scenic as well, but not like this. It's as though the hills and valleys here are carpeted in green velvet."

"Yes, Ireland is truly beautiful. I've come to love it. But I'll let you in on a little secret," Patrick said with a twinkle in his eye. "There's a reason why Ireland is so green: It rains all the time. To do God's work here means that you'll be constantly walking and preaching in the rain. I can't tell you how many times I've been drenched to the skin, shivering in the cold wind. My feet are often so caked with mud I can't tell for sure if my toes are still there."

"But at least your hut, as modest as it is, keeps the rain out," Auxilius observed.

"Yes, that it does. Now, if I could only find a way to take it with me when I go to preach," Patrick commented with a chuckle. "But now, tell me the news about Britain. How are things there?"

The two men hesitated for a moment. Finally, Secundinus spoke up. "As you know, Britain enjoyed a period of peace for several years, brought about by the Saxons."

"Yes. Vortigern convinced the people that our only chance for peace was to invite the Saxons to come and settle between us and the Picts. I said it would never work—that it was putting our trust in alliances with idol-worshiping pagans. But so far, it looks like I was wrong."

"No, you weren't wrong," Secundinus countered. "The Saxon peace lasted for several years. But finally the Saxons grew tired of having only a strip of buffer land in northern Britain for themselves. Once they observed how weak and demoralized the Britons were, they realized they could have the whole island for themselves. So they sent word to their fellow Saxons back on the Jutland Peninsula, telling them of the situation. They invited the other Saxons, as well as the neighboring Angles, to come and help them take all of Britain. Once their comrades arrived, the Saxons allied themselves with the Picts and turned their vicious swords on the Christians of Britain."

"Oh, no!" Patrick moaned, burying his head in his hands. "If only the people had trusted in God and returned to Him."

"The Saxons swept across the countryside of northern and eastern Britain, killing, raping, and burning," Secundinus continued in a sad voice. "They even burst into churches in the middle of worship and cut down the presbyters and bishops in the middle of their prayers." Patrick was now openly crying.

Overcome with emotion, Secundinus could not continue, so Auxilius took over the narration. "The Britons have quickly found that the Saxons are far worse to have as enemies than the Scots and Picts put together. The Saxons take no prisoners and show no mercy on account of age, rank, or sex. They burn whole families alive in their houses. Anyone who flees from the flames is caught and butchered on the spot. In fact, the Saxons usually leave no survivors to bury the dead. Everywhere, dead bodies rot, filling the land with a horrid stench."

"Hasn't anyone escaped?" Patrick asked in a broken voice.

"A few have," Secundinus answered, having recovered his composure. "They flee to the mountains and forests, where they eke out a wretched existence, living in constant fear for their lives. Others seek refuge in the villages and cities in western Britain, which has not yet fallen to the Angles and Saxons."

"It's a wonder that anyone's left," Auxilius added. "Between the Scots and Picts from the north, the Irish raiders from the west, and the Saxons in the east, it's as though all of Britain is in the stranglehold of an evil giant. When news reached Gaul of the horrible conditions in Britain, we sailed to the western coast of Britain to see what we could do to help the Christians there."

"And how are things there, on the west coast?" Patrick inquired anxiously.

"Not good," Secundinus answered. "Refugees from all over the country are pouring into the coastal cities and villages. As a result, the cities and villages are overcrowded and one plague after another has swept over them. The fury of the plagues is as deadly as that of the Saxons."

"Did you by any chance visit the village of Bannavem Taburniae?" Patrick asked with a disturbed look. "That's where I'm from."

"Yes, that's where we learned about you and your mission."

"What about my parents? Did you meet them perchance?"

Secundinus hesitated, obviously not wanting to answer. "Patrick, I'm sorry to be the one to have to tell you. B–but–they're both dead–from the plague."

Patrick was silent for a moment. He then excused himself so he could have some time in solitude. He told his guests to make themselves at home, while he took a walk in the nearby hills to come to grips with the news he had just heard. While he was out, Lomman dropped by.

"Hello. I'm Secundinus, and this is Auxilius, from Britain," Secundinus greeted him. "Well, actually, we're originally from Gaul. We've come to help in the work here."

"Wonderful!" Lomman exclaimed, embracing the two men. "I'm Lomman."

"Lomman? Yes, we've heard about you. You're one of the original men who came here with Patrick, aren't you?"

"Yes, I am. By the way, where is Patrick?"

The men filled Lomman in on the events in Britain and the death of Patrick's parents. "We didn't even get a chance to tell Patrick that after the death of his parents, an uncle was appointed executor. He sold all of the property and deposited the proceeds with the local presbyters. They, in turn, have entrusted those goods with us. We've brought them for Patrick. Perhaps he can build a more comfortable place with them or something."

"Not Patrick," Lomman sighed. "Knowing him, he'll use it all to fund the work of evangelism. We don't receive much aid from Britain anymore. Of course, with the way things are in Britain, I well understand why they can't send more aid. But tell me, has this time of calamity brought the people of Britain closer to God?"

"I'm afraid not," Auxilius answered sadly, shaking his head. "From what I've been told, when the Saxons first turned on the Britons, the people cried out to God with upraised arms and great lamentation. But when no answer from God was forthcoming, the people decided that their only deliverance would be in the sword, not the church. Their hastily organized armies now fight valiantly against the Saxons. Yet, they've lost battle after battle. The Saxons continue their butchery with seeming invincibility."

"You mean no one has ever successfully fought the Saxons?" Lomman asked.

"Up to now, no," Auxilius replied. "Unless God intervenes, there may no longer be a Britain in a few years. With what has happened, the people have almost totally lost their faith in God. The majority of the people don't even attend church anymore. Many are openly worshiping the idols of their ancestors."

"I mean no offense by this, but I'm surprised you didn't stay in Britain," Lomman interjected. "I mean, with things being in the state they are right now."

"Well, we would have," explained Secundinus, "if there were a shortage of leaders there. However, right now, there's an abundance of shepherds. The bishops, presbyters, and deacons have all stayed in the church. It's just the flocks that have dwindled. Our efforts to revive the people met with no success at all."

"So after considerable prayer," Auxilius added, "we felt that God would have us labor where the harvest is great. Ireland seems to be that place right now."

"That it is!" Lomman heartily agreed. "Listen, I'm leaving tomorrow on a short preaching trip. Why don't the two of you come with me, so you can see firsthand what God is doing here." The visitors readily agreed, and the next morning, they set off on foot with Lomman and some others. It rained the whole day, and a chilly Atlantic wind quickly had Secundinus and Auxilius shivering.

"Patrick warned us that it rains all the time here in Ireland," Secundinus remarked, drawing his hood over his head.

"Yes, it does," Lomman readily acknowledged. "But you'll rarely hear Patrick complain about it. Quite often when he's preaching, he's forced to sleep out in the rain or in crude temporary huts, which don't keep the rain out. And he's not a young man anymore. He's nearly sixty, you know. Although he seldom says anything, I can tell from watching him that his body constantly aches. I've seen him spend many a night lying on the cold ground, shaking with fever chills."

"Before we came to Britain, we had never even heard of Patrick," Secundinus commented. "But he sounds like an incredible man of God."

"He definitely is, and the people of Ireland know it. His reputation precedes him when he sets out to preach. Everywhere he goes, people fall at his feet. When he speaks, crowds of people are nearly always converted."

"It sounds like he's become their national hero," Auxilius chimed in.

"Yes, that's exactly right. You see, the Irish strongly relate to a hero figure. They have no written laws and very little concept of an organized government like we do. Instead, they rally around their heroes. From the very first, Patrick has steered the people toward Jesus Christ as their new hero, and they have responded marvelously to that concept. Yet the people also need a physical, flesh-and-blood model they can see with their eyes."

"And Patrick has become that flesh-and-blood hero," Secundinus submitted.

"Exactly. The Irish can *hear* about Christ. But Patrick, they can *see*. Like Paul, Patrick has been able to say to the Irish, 'Become imitators of me, as even I imitate Christ.' I've never met anyone who walks so closely in the footsteps of Jesus as Patrick does."

"I'm beginning to like this Patrick," Auxilius responded. "Give us some examples of what you mean by his walking in the footsteps of Jesus."

"To begin with, Jesus never married. Neither has Patrick. Jesus had no house to call his home. Neither does Patrick—unless you want to count his little hut made of sticks and mud. Besides his clothes, Jesus had practically no material possessions. Neither does Patrick. Jesus loved and forgave His enemies. So has Patrick."

"What enemies are you talking about?" Secundinus asked.

"Did you know that Patrick had originally been kidnapped by the Irish as a lad of sixteen?"

The two newcomers looked surprised. "No, no one ever told us that," Secundinus admitted.

"Well, he was. He served as a slave here in Ireland for six years. As a result, he missed out on his education. Through God's intervention, he finally escaped from Ireland. But he bore no hatred for his kidnappers. Instead, when God called him to come here to bring the love of Christ to these people, he responded without hesitation. Now he prays that God will let him die in Ireland."

"Has Patrick had any other enemies?" Auxilius asked as he sat down on a boulder to rest.

"Oh yes. He's had *plenty*, both inside and outside the church. In fact, even his best friend betrayed him."

"Really? Tell us about this betrayal," Secundinus asked.

So Lomman told the men about Patrick's false friend, Marcus, and the treacherous thing he had done. "Yet, the entire time we've been in Ireland, I've never heard Patrick say even one unkind word about Marcus," Lomman concluded.

The men continued their journey. "Have I told you what a man of prayer Patrick is?" Lomman asked.

"No," the other two chorused.

"Let me tell you, he prays like no one I've ever met before. He spends entire days at a time in prayer. And he constantly fasts. I think that's why God has protected him–and the rest of us–from the continual dangers we face."

"What sort of dangers?" Auxilius asked nervously.

"Well, from the moment Patrick and the rest of us set foot in Ireland, our lives have been constantly in danger. You see, Ireland is fragmented into many different clans. I hear there's about two hundred of them. And these clans are constantly waging petty wars against each other. So it's highly dangerous for a band of foreigners to travel about the countryside, journeying from clan to clan."

"But it didn't seem dangerous there in Armagh," Auxilius noted.

"That's right," Lomman answered. "But that's because of the effects of the Gospel. However, when you venture into places where the Gospel has never been preached, it's a very different story. If you're not careful, one of the chieftains will kidnap you and either hold you for ransom or sell you as a slave."

Secundinus and Auxilius glanced at each other anxiously. "So how do you manage to preach the Gospel?" Secundinus inquired with a puzzled brow.

"Well, since Patrick knew the customs in advance, from his years here as a slave, he pays tribute to each chieftain in order to travel freely through his territory. Of course, this can get to be expensive. We've exhausted all our resources in doing this. And no doubt Patrick will spend his entire inheritance in the same way."

"But once you pay tribute to a chieftain, it ensures your safety, right?" Secundinus asked, swallowing hard.

"Usually it does. But not always. About a year ago, Patrick and I had just paid a handsome tribute demanded by Coirpre, one of the Irish kings. In return, Coirpre guaranteed us and our men safe passage throughout his territory. He even sent his sons along to give us protection. However, we hadn't journeyed far before the king's sons pounced on us and stole everything we had."

"Oh, no!" Auxilius interjected.

"But that's not all," Lomman continued. "They then took us to their father's house, where we were all put in iron chains. In fact, the king was planning to kill all of us, but our time had not yet come. Although the rest of us were all terribly frightened, Patrick's faith never wavered. He prayed day and night to God, hardly taking time to eat and drink. Suddenly, two weeks later, Coirpre released us and even returned all of our property."

"What happened to make him change his mind?" Auxilius asked eagerly.

"Well, about a week after kidnapping us, two of his sons were killed in battle. Coirpre felt that God had punished him for the treacherous way he had dealt with us. So that's why he let us go."

"But that was an isolated incident, right?" Secundinus asked.

"No, I'm afraid that things like that are the norm. I don't mean that most kings go back on their word of honor. Very few do. Rather, what I mean is that without God's hand of protection, Patrick and I wouldn't have lasted more than a week in Ireland. Even now, we daily expect murder, deceit, captivity, or some other thing. Eleven years ago, Rome sent a man here named Palladius. He lasted only a year and then left."

Seeing the countenances of the two men, Lomman added, "I hope I haven't discouraged you. But I do think you should know the truth about our work here. It's a hard life."

"No, you haven't discouraged us," Secundinus replied, glancing at Auxilius for confirmation. "The things you've said are a bit disturbing, of course. But we weren't expecting an easy time when we decided to come here."

"Furthermore," Auxilius added, "it's a bit exciting to think about working alongside a man of faith like Patrick."

"Yes it is," Lomman agreed. "Patrick came here to die. Before he ever set foot in Ireland, he cast himself into the hands of God Almighty. His life is totally in God's hands. I don't know how long he has left here. Tomorrow may be his last day. Or perhaps God wants him to continue working for another twenty or thirty years. Only He knows."

"Let's hope it's for another twenty or thirty years," Auxilius remarked.

"Amen. The others and I have a lot of maturing to do before we'll be ready to take over the work here," Lomman agreed.

By this time, the men had reached their destination. A crowd had already gathered, having heard that a man sent by Patrick was coming to tell them about this new King, Jesus. Before the week was over, Lomman and the others had baptized more than forty people. When they returned to Patrick's hut at Armagh a few weeks later, Secundinus and Auxilius couldn't help remarking over and over how they had never seen such a marvelous response to the Gospel.

"Yes, the fields are definitely ripe for harvest here," Patrick agreed. "God will be able to use both of you in a powerful way, so long as you stay close to Him and do everything in His strength, not your own. But you should also know that not everyone in Ireland is receptive to the Gospel. We've made some powerful enemies here."

"Yes, we've heard about them," Auxilius replied.

Pointing to a worn Bible laying on a nearby table, Patrick asked Secundinus to hand it to him. Then, turning to Paul's second epistle to the Corinthians, he read to them this passage: 'In journeys often, in perils of waters, in perils of robbers, in perils of my own countrymen, in perils of the Gentiles, in perils in the city, in perils in the wilderness, in perils in the sea, in perils among false brethren; in weariness and toil, in sleeplessness often, in hunger and thirst, in fastings often, in cold and nakedness.'"[1]

Closing the Bible, Patrick looked at the two men and added, "That describes our life in Ireland—which is now your life as well."[2]

---

[1] 2 Cor. 11:26, 27.

[2] *Confessio* §51-55, 59; *Ecclesiastical History* §15.

Eighteen

A Man of Integrity

"I can't help but notice that a striking number of your converts here are totally on fire for the Lord," Secundinus commented to Patrick one day.

"Yes, through God's grace, they are. But it would be a mistake to imagine that all of our converts are exemplary Christians. Even the apostles had plenty of backsliders, lukewarm Christians, and false brethren among their converts. It's no different here."

"What do you do when people backslide?" Secundinus asked.

"I refuse to water down Christ's standards in order to make Christianity fit into pagan Irish culture. When men and women return to fighting, drunkenness, and licentiousness, I rebuke them severely. If they don't repent, I excommunicate them without hesitation."

"It sounds like you're a strong disciplinarian."

"I am. But so were the apostles. And you'll have to be one, too, or else you'll see your work here destroyed by Satan. Never wink at sin. At the same time, always temper your discipline with love and mercy. Remember, the purpose of discipline is to save souls—not to vent anger."

"I have to admit that I'm rather surprised that the Irish submit to your excommunications," Auxilius remarked as he examined a scrape on his leg. "I would have thought that they would threaten you, or at least refuse to accept it."

"Well, I have to admit that Irish culture has helped me a lot. In Ireland, the most powerful persons are not the kings, as you might expect."

"Really? Who are they, then?" Secundinus inquired.

"The Druids," Patrick replied. "The Druids are the lawmakers and judges of all disputes. If a man doesn't accept their judgments—even if he's a king—he and his entire family will be banned from all religious rites and sacred functions."

"But you're not a Druid," Auxilius observed. "So how does that help you?"

"Well, as a somewhat natural thing, the Irish give me and other Christian leaders the status that Druids enjoy in their society. This has greatly facilitated the spread of the Gospel, since the Irish are used to submitting to their religious leaders. When I have to excommunicate someone, it's not something strange to the Irish. Of course, I always try to be fair-handed in my discipline, treating wealthy and poor alike."

One Saturday afternoon, Patrick was elated to see a delegation of British clergy standing outside his hut. He embraced them all warmly and invited them in. He was particularly surprised to see Quintus among the group.

"Did you receive our letter?" Quintus asked.

"Yes, I did. It arrived just a few days ago. Auxilius brought it to me. I was so happy to hear that you were coming to visit and would be bringing some supplies for the work here."

"Yes, we've heard that you've had a limited amount of success here," Quintus commented.

"A *limited* amount?" Patrick responded. "Why, the floodgates have opened. The Irish are flocking to the church by the thousands. Oh, but the credit doesn't go to me. It's God who's doing everything."

"I see," Quintus said dryly.

That night, Patrick and his companions enjoyed a simple meal with the delegates from Britain. "How are things in Britain these days?" Patrick asked, with a look of concern on his face. "Secundinus and Auxilius have filled us in on what the Saxons have treacherously done. Has there been any change?"

"As a matter of fact, there has. Britain finally has a hero, someone who can defeat the Saxons," Quintus announced proudly.

"What's his name?" Patrick asked curiously.

"Coroticus."

Patrick shook his head. "I don't think I've ever heard of him. Who is he?"

"He rules a small kingdom on the west coast of Britain," one of the presbyters explained. "He and his soldiers have met the Saxons in battle several times and have soundly defeated them each time. It looks like he has delivered us from the hands of our enemies."

"You mean he's driving the Saxons out of Britain?" Patrick asked in astonishment.

"No, they're too strong for anyone to do that. But Coroticus has halted their advance. What's more, he's entered into a peace treaty with the Scots and the Picts. As a result, the people on the west coast of Britain are filled with a new spirit of hope. Now, if Coroticus can just do something about these cursed Irish devils who continue to harass us from the sea."

After communion the next morning, an Irish king walked up to the front of the church with an ornate wooden box, filled with jewels of all sorts. He then placed it on the altar. Patrick was standing by the altar, and he immediately picked the box up and handed it back to the king, speaking to him in Gaelic.

"What was that all about?" Quintus asked a few minutes later.

"That was Mac Fechach, an Irish king. I excommunicated him last month for adultery."

"So what were the jewels for?" one of the presbyters queried.

"He wanted to make a gift of them to the church, but I refused them. I have made it an absolute policy that I do not accept gifts or alms from excommunicated Christians."

"What!" Quintus exclaimed. "You mean you turned down a generous gift like that? Why, that gift would have provided you with the funds to carry on your mission."

The other presbyters all nodded their heads in agreement. "Let me remind you," Quintus continued crossly, "that Britain can't finance your work indefinitely. I could tell that this king—what did you say his name was?"

"Mac Fechach."

"Yes, well this Mac Fechach was obviously offended. Years ago, I had seriously questioned whether you had the wisdom to take on a work as important as this. Now I can plainly see that you don't. Turning down funds that God has provided for your work! I'm going to report this to the bishops back in Britain."

"Please try to understand," Patrick urged Quintus and the others in a conciliatory tone. "I appreciate your concerns. However, I well know that gifts from sinners come with a price tag. If I accept gifts from excommunicated kings, eventually the church here will come to rely upon those gifts to finance its ministry. Before long, we'll be bending our teachings in order not to offend such people."

"We accept gifts from excommunicated persons in Britain," Quintus retorted frostily. "Are you saying that you know better than we do?"

"I pass no judgment at all on what you do in Britain. I'm only saying this is what I believe is best for the church in Ireland."

"We'll talk more about this some other time," Quintus replied stiffly and then turned and walked out of the church, followed by the other British clergymen.

The next day, the group of British presbyters spoke to Patrick again. "We've discussed this among ourselves, and we've decided that you must change your policy here concerning gifts from excommunicated persons. We feel that when they give gifts to the church, it shows their repentance. To refuse their gift is the same as refusing to forgive them."

"What about the poor, who can't give such gifts?" Patrick replied. "Am I to have a double standard here between the rich and the poor?"

"Do you really think you know more about governing the

church than we do?" Quintus countered, his face flushed with anger. "We've decided you must go and apologize to king what's-his-name at once, and we'll accompany you. Perhaps he's still willing to make his gift to the church."

"I'm sorry, but I can't do that," Patrick replied resolutely.

"Apparently you don't understand us," Quintus insisted, raising his voice. "We're not *asking* you to apologize to the king. We're *ordering* you to do so—at once."

Patrick stood silently for a moment, staring Quintus in the eye. "The entire time I was in Britain, I obeyed my clergy. For twenty-five years, while thousands of these poor Irish people were dying daily without Christ, I remained in Britain because the leaders of the church said I couldn't go. But now God has opened the door for me to minister here. You no longer have any standing to order me to do anything. Since when do a group of presbyters presume to order a bishop to do anything?" Patrick glared at the presbyters in exasperation.

"Pulling rank on us, is that it?" Quintus shot back testily.

"No, God has pulled rank on you." With that, Patrick turned his back and walked away.

The next day, when the delegation of British clergy were about to leave, Patrick quickly came over to them. "Listen, I want to apologize for the way I spoke to you yesterday," he began. "You've come all the way from Britain to see me, and I'm afraid I haven't been a very good host. Please forgive me; I'd love to have you stay longer. Let's not quarrel."

"So then you've changed your mind about the king?" one of the men asked.

"No, I'm truly sorry, but I can't do what you've asked. But let's not allow that to put a wall between us. I genuinely do respect your counsel and try to follow it whenever I can."

Some of the men came forward and warmly embraced Patrick, apologizing for what had happened. But not Quintus. He simply stared icily at Patrick. Finally, he broke the silence. Turning to Secundinus and Auxilius, he said, "We can't order you to come back with us. However, in light of what has happened, we feel that's what you should do. We simply cannot recommend your staying here any longer to work with Patrick. God can well use you in Britain. We must leave at once, or we'll miss our boat."

"Thank you for your concern," Secundinus replied. "However, this is where I believe God has called me to work. So I'm going to stay." Auxilius quickly indicated that his sentiments were the same. With that, the British delegates turned and left.

Patrick's eyes sadly watched the delegates disappear into the gray Irish fog. "I'm sorry that our meeting had to be like this," he said, turning to Secundinus and Auxilius. "You probably think me a stubborn old man."

"To the contrary. We've seen first hand that your policy on gifts is right," Secundinus interjected. "In Gaul, the church often accepts gifts from ungodly kings and queens. After that, the church is afraid to ever excommunicate or rebuke them. I believe it will eventually be the undoing of the church in Europe."[1]

---

[1] *Confessio* §37, 49; *Epistolo* §8, 11, 12.

Nineteen

A Day of Infamy

It was a pleasant summer day. Secundinus and Auxilius had proved to be able missionaries and were now preaching in other parts of Ireland. In a meadow overlooking a sandy beach on the east coast of Ireland, Patrick and Lomman were leading a group of new believers in fasting and prayer. These new converts were readying themselves for baptism the next morning. With bowed heads, tearful eyes, and contrite hearts, they confessed their sins and prayed to God for forgiveness. The vigil lasted well into the night.

At dawn the next morning, Patrick and Lomman led the group down to the beach and baptized them in the chilly waters of the Irish Sea. As was his usual practice, Patrick laid hands on the newly baptized believers, clothed them in white robes, and traced the sign of the cross on their foreheads with scented oil.

Patrick and Lomman had an appointment at another church, so they left the group of new believers under the care of Ailbe, a young Irish presbyter. As they watched Patrick and his companions disappear into the nearby forest, the group of new converts praised God and sang Psalms and hymns together. They ended their pre-baptismal fast with a simple meal of bread, fish, and parched grain. A few hours after Patrick and Lomman had left, one of the newly baptized men spied a ship approaching. As the ship drew closer, they recognized it to be a Roman ship.

"It must be from Britain!" one of them exclaimed jubilantly. "No doubt it brings more supplies and workers for the church in

Ireland."

Indeed, the boat *was* from Britain, and as it came closer to shore, the Irish converts could see the cross emblazoned on its main sail. Several of the men in the boat leaped into the water with ropes in their hands, wading to shore, pulling the boat behind them.

"Let's go help them unload their provisions," one of the newly baptized Christians suggested. So the entire party of men and women hurried excitedly down to the shore. As they drew closer to the ship, these new believers were surprised to find that the sailors were all armed with swords and spears. However, they shrugged it off, thinking that the sailors feared attacks from pirates.

Ailbe led the party of new believers toward the boat. "I wish Patrick were here," he told the others nervously. "I can't speak British and I know only a little Latin."

"Welcome, brothers!" Ailbe called out in imperfect Latin. With outstretched arms, he approached one of the visitors. Just as he was about to embrace the visitor, the man replied coldly, "You're not *my* brother." He suddenly unsheathed his sword and plunged it into Ailbe's stomach. The young presbyter staggered back in astonishment and then collapsed, blood gushing out of his gaping wound.

The other Irish Christians stood frozen in terror and disbelief. *Patrick said that Christians love one another.* Suddenly they began screaming and praying aloud to God. As they turned to run, the soldiers fell upon them mercilessly with naked swords and iron-tipped javelins.

"That's for my daughter," one of the soldiers grunted as he hacked a young Irishman to death. Another soldier hurled a spear into the back of a fleeing man. A third soldier grabbed one of the women by her long red hair and yanked her to the ground. In a few moments' time, the soldiers had captured all of the women and boys and had butchered nearly all of the men. A few of the men escaped into the woods, running in terror.

One group of soldiers then dashed quickly towards some houses they saw in the distance. When they reached the houses, they brutally massacred everyone in sight and carried off as many valuables as they could find. Before leaving the houses, they set them on fire. In less than two hours, it was all over. The soldiers were back on the ship, which was now loaded with prisoners and loot. They then quickly set off for Britain.

Meanwhile, the Irish Christians who had escaped caught up with Patrick. Worn out from their run, they collapsed at his feet. Gasping for air as they spoke, they told him what had happened. Their words cut through Patrick like the iron blade of one of the soldiers' swords.

"Quick, we must hurry back before the ship leaves!" Patrick shouted to Lomman. He and some of the men immediately set out on foot for the coast, at the speed of a forced march. "God, give my frail legs the strength they had when I was young," Patrick prayed silently as he pushed on. "Father, please don't let the ship leave before we arrive."

When they finally reached the meadow by the sea, Patrick stood aghast in horror. The bright green grass was strewn with the bodies of the slain Christian men. They still wore their baptismal robes, which were now stained in crimson. Falling prostrate, Patrick wept profusely, crying aloud, "My newborn children! My newborn children! If only I had died instead of you. My poor children, my poor children."

Tears still streaming from his eyes, Patrick knelt down by one of the slain men. He was a young man of about twenty, with reddish-brown hair and green eyes. The scent of myrrh was still on his forehead. Patrick gently cradled the man's head on his lap. "Why? Father, why?" Patrick yelled out to the heavens. "Why did my newborn children have to die like this?"

Patrick mourned at length until he realized that none of the women had been slain. "The women," he cried out. "They've taken the women captive! They'll sell them as slaves. Quick, we must catch up with them before it's too late. Lomman, run and find some of the brothers and get a boat." Lomman and some of the other men quickly scurried off to do as Patrick said.

"Bring back some writing supplies with you as well," Patrick yelled.

Patrick and the remaining men then set to work to bury the bodies of the dead Christians. The others returned in a few hours with a boat and some writing materials. Patrick sat down on a nearby boulder, hurriedly wrote out a letter, and sealed it. "Here," he said to Lomman. "Take this letter with you and sail at once for Britain. The letter orders the soldiers to immediately release the captives to you and to return the stolen property." Lomman took the letter in hand and left at once for Britain, taking a worker from Britain with him.

"At least we can save the women and boys," Patrick consoled himself as he watched the small currach[1] disappear on the gray Irish Sea.[2]

---

[1]A light, skin-covered boat.

[2]*Epistolo* §2-4, 12, 15, 16.

Twenty

Jesus or Barabbas?

Patrick would have been quite surprised at the reception the raiders received when they returned to Britain. The man who had raided Ireland was none other than Coroticus, Britain's new hero. Instead of being treated like murdering pirates, they were welcomed as champions! These men were their saviors! To the cheers of adoring throngs, Coroticus and his men marched their captives down the road to their fortress, an abandoned Roman garrison, and chained them in the courtyard. That night, Coroticus and his soldiers celebrated their "victory" in a drunken revelry.

The next morning, Lomman arrived from Ireland. He ran up to the first person he saw, a fisherman drying his nets. "Something terrible has happened!" he cried in alarm. "Some men from Britain raided the coast of Ireland, killing scores of innocent Christian men and taking captive a large group of innocent Christian women and boys."

The fisherman continued working with his nets, not answering at first. He finally paused and asked dryly, "Were these men who were killed Irish or British?"

"Why they were Irish, of course."

"And these women and boys who were captured—were *they* Irish or British?"

"Irish. But I don't see what..."

"Well, then, they weren't innocent!" the fisherman croaked.

"What do you mean, 'they weren't innocent'?" Lomman demanded. "They were all newly baptized Christians. They've never harmed anyone."

"They're guilty by association," the fisherman snapped. "The Irish have been plundering our coast for as long as I can remember. My brother was kidnapped by them. But Coroticus has finally taught them a lesson. 'An eye for an eye and a tooth for a tooth' is what I say."

"So it was Coroticus who did this?" Lomman burst out.

"That's right. King Coroticus, the savior of the British. He predicted that he would catch the Irish by surprise if he raided them. He was definitely right. I bet the Irish will think twice about raiding us again after what he did to them."

"I've got to talk to him," Lomman insisted anxiously. "Where's his fortress?"

"You take the coastal road to the north. His castle is about six miles up the road. You can't miss it. But don't be thinking you're going to get any sympathy from him or from any of the rest of us."

Arriving at the fortress that afternoon, Lomman boldly handed Patrick's letter to one of Coroticus' officers. The man read the letter and broke out in a derisive laugh.

"Listen to this. This man wants us to turn over all of our captives and booty to him." The other soldiers roared in laughter, slapping each other on their backs and jeering at Lomman and his companion.

One of the soldiers stepped forward, made a sweeping bow, and then said mockingly, "Why, of course, we'll turn everything over to you. We risked our lives to obtain these slaves and goods. But that doesn't matter. We'll do whatever this bishop of the Irish demands of us." The soldier then slapped Lomman across his face. "You traitorous, holier-than-thou hypocrite! You and your dog of a bishop just want these slaves and goods for yourselves. Now, get out of here, before we sell you as a slave, too."

Lomman stared at the soldier for a moment, his piercing eyes probing the soul of this professing Christian. He then abruptly turned, and he and his companion stormed out of the courtyard and headed back to Ireland.

Lomman looked back at the coast as it disappeared from sight. "It's just like Secundinus told us," he said sadly to the other man, who was manning the steering oar. "Christianity in Britain has sunk so low it can hardly be called Christianity any more. I would never have believed that professing Christians would sell their innocent brothers and sisters as slaves to the evil Picts."

Patrick shook his head in disbelief when his men reported to him what had happened in Britain. "I knew our people had wandered far from God," he lamented, "but I never dreamed things were this bad. Coroticus is nothing but a cold-blooded murderer. If only the Spirit would allow me to return to Britain, I would confront this Coroticus face-to-face. But I have spoken to God too many times already about that, and He won't permit me to return to Britain. The only thing left for me to do is to excommunicate Coroticus and his soldiers and trust that this will bring them to repentance."

Patrick retired to the hut where he was staying and prayed at length about the matter. Several times, he broke down and sobbed as he cried out to God. Lomman came in to comfort him.

"I don't know whether I'm grieving more for the slain men or for the female captives who have been violated and by now are the concubines of pagan men," Patrick told Lomman with a hoarse voice. "Maybe I grieve the most for Coroticus and his soldiers—and the British people who support them. For they've exchanged their eternal souls for their temporal earthly lives."

After considerable prayer, Patrick picked up a writing tablet and sat down at the rough wooden table in his hut to write the letter of excommunication. "Oh, that I could write in vivid prose, instead of my crude Latin," he complained.

"Don't worry about your grammar," Lomman encouraged him. "Just make sure the message is powerful."

"Indeed, it must be," Patrick agreed. "The issue at stake here is enormous. Either the kingdom of God is a real kingdom that transcends all boundaries of nationality and race—or else it's an illusion. If it's an illusion, Christianity is no better than the pagan religions. Paul said that the kingdom of God becomes nothing when Christians take each other to court. What would he say about Christians *slaughtering* other Christians—merely because they belong to a different nation?"

Patrick was quiet for a moment and then began writing, "I, Patrick, an uneducated sinner, live in Ireland. I am a bishop. I believe beyond a doubt that what I am is only by the grace of God. And so I live among barbarians—a pilgrim and expatriate because of God's love. I never wanted to have to write a letter that is so severe and harsh as this. However, the love of God and truth of Christ have wrenched these words from me."[1]

Patrick hesitated for a moment. He weighed the consequences of what he was about to say. He felt the pain of each word as though it were a dagger thrust into his heart. Asking God for strength, he continued, "I have written these words with my own hand, to be delivered to Coroticus and his soldiers. I do not say, to my fellow citizens. Nor do I say to fellow citizens of the holy Romans. Rather, I say to fellow citizens *of the demons*! I say this because of their evil works. Like all enemies of Christ, they live in death. They are allies of the Scots and the pagan Picts. Dripping with blood, they wallow in the blood of innocent Christians—Christians whom I have begotten into the assembly of God and confirmed in Christ!"[2]

Patrick's heart pounded as he kept writing, describing how Coroticus and his men had butchered innocent, newly baptized Christians. "Father, please help me find the right words," he prayed silently as he continued to write.

"Let every God-fearing man know that Coroticus and his soldiers are enemies of me and of Christ my God, for whom I am an ambassador. Murderers! Ravening wolves who devour the

---

[1]Patrick *Epistolo* §1.

[2]Ibid. §2.

people of the Lord as they would devour bread! Therefore, I urge you with all earnestness—you who are holy and humble of heart—that it is not permissible to fellowship with such people. Nor to partake of a meal with them. You must not even accept their alms. Not until these men are reconciled to God, through tears and sorrow and repentance. And not until they bring back from the Scots and Picts the baptized servants and handmaids of Christ, for whom He died and was crucified."[1]

Patrick dropped his pen, fell to his knees, and wept. "Father, forgive me for writing such a strong letter. But please let it penetrate their hearts and bring repentance." He signed the letter, sealed it, and carried it to Auxilius to take to Britain.

"Come right back as soon as you deliver the letter," he warned Auxilius. "The situation could quickly become dangerous." Auxilius assured him he would.

Arriving in Britain the next day, Auxilius delivered the letter to one of the local presbyters, asking him to read it to Coroticus in front of all the people. After Auxilius left, the presbyter first read the letter himself. Visibly disturbed by its contents, he quickly told the other clergymen and the community leaders about it. They all suggested that he take it to Bishop Julius. Before long, news of the letter had traveled up and down the western coast of Britain, causing quite a sensation. Bishop Julius quickly convened a meeting of all of the British clergy in the area.

"We're in a real dilemma," Julius told the group of clergymen. "The vast majority of our congregations are solidly behind Coroticus. If we uphold Patrick's excommunication, the consequences will be severe. At a minimum, we will lose a large segment of our parishioners, perhaps the majority of those who still come to church. At worst, the people might riot and kill us. It's happened before in other countries."

"Who does this upstart bishop think he is, anyway?" Quintus roared indignantly, rising to his feet. "He can't excommunicate

---

[1]Ibid §7,12.

one of our kings!"

"Yes, but to ignore the letter of excommunication would weaken church discipline," another presbyter objected. "It would also mean turning our backs on a bishop whom we've ordained."

"Patrick has no jurisdiction here," Quintus countered. "He was specifically ordained as the bishop of the Irish. He won't accept our input into his work there, so there's no reason we should accept his meddling in our affairs here."

"That's right!" another presbyter agreed. "If we excommunicate Coroticus and his soldiers, who's going to protect us from the Saxons and the Picts? Patrick certainly won't defend us." The group of men chuckled at this last remark.

Bishop Julius stood up and quieted the group. "Are we all in agreement then that we ignore Patrick's letter of excommunication?" The crowd of clergymen noisily indicated their agreement. "Coroticus, not Patrick!" many of them began shouting.

Finally, Bishop Brannoc rose slowly to his feet, being helped by several attendants. He was eighty years old now and was nearly blind. Because of his age and health, he was quite limited in his ministerial functions. But his love of God had not diminished. He spoke in a hoarse, quivering voice. "Let's not deceive ourselves," he told the group. "It's not Coroticus we've chosen over Patrick. It's Barabbas we've chosen over Jesus."

"What do you mean?" one man asked.

"I'm saying that we're faced with the same choice that was before the crowd in Jerusalem in Jesus' day. Would they choose Jesus or Barabbas? In Jesus, they had a man who preached about the kingdom of *heaven*, not a kingdom on earth. He wouldn't deliver His people from their Roman conquerors, but instead He told them to love their enemies. In contrast, in Barabbas, the people had a man of action, a political revolutionary. He wasn't content to wait for the kingdom of heaven. In Barabbas, the Jews saw a hero who might deliver them from the hated Romans. In Jesus, they had only promises. So the crowd chose Barabbas."

"But that's different from our situation," Quintus objected.

"Is it really?" Brannoc countered. "In Patrick, we have a man who preaches the kingdom of heaven. A man who loves the enemies of Britain and has devoted his life to them. A man who trusts only in God, not the sword. In Coroticus, we have a man who can deliver us from our enemies. Yet, we all know in our hearts that he's an ungodly man. When he's not killing Saxons or Irish, he's usually drunk or in bed with one of the maidens who fawn over him. Now, he's murdered innocent Christian men and sold innocent Christian women to be the concubines of the Picts. If we choose him over Patrick, we are indeed choosing Barabbas over Jesus."

"Nonsense!" Quintus objected loudly, jumping to his feet again. "Patrick is no Jesus, and Coroticus is no Barabbas. God obviously has blessed Coroticus, or he would never have been able to defeat the Saxons. In contrast, Patrick is nothing more than a self-righteous, self-promoting hypocrite! We all know the awful thing he did when he was a young man. That reveals his real character. He's only in Ireland for personal gain. If the people knew the kind of things he's doing over in Ireland, they would curse the very mention of his name."

"What kind of things?" someone asked from the crowd.

"For one thing, he charges fees to baptize or ordain anyone. While the other presbyters and I were over there, we witnessed this firsthand. One of their kings brought to Patrick a wooden chest loaded with gold and jewels. It was a baptismal payment. However, Patrick haughtily rejected it, saying it wasn't enough. He told the king to come back with more, or else he wouldn't baptize him."

"You never said anything about that before," Brannoc interrupted in a quavering voice.

"Well–I–uh, didn't want to disillusion the people. They're already weak in faith. If they knew that a bishop was doing these things, it might destroy what little faith they have left. So I kept quiet for their sake. Now, I see that I was wrong to cover this up." With a gesture toward the group, Quintus added, "If you don't believe what I'm saying, ask the other presbyters; they were with me."

The other presbyters all nodded their heads in agreement. "Not only that," one of the presbyters exclaimed, "Patrick is also teaching heresy over there. Just like Pelagius, he's saying that we can be saved without the grace of God, and all sorts of other heretical teachings."

Bishop Julius now arose. "Well, I think this settles the matter. Patrick has no jurisdiction here. In fact, if anyone's going to be excommunicated, it should probably be him."

The false accusations against Patrick quickly spread through the townspeople, and before long his name was being vilified all up and down the west coast of Britain.

A few months later, one of Patrick's assistants sailed to Britain to obtain some needed supplies. While there, he learned what was being said about Patrick. When Patrick heard the news, he was utterly crushed. For several months, he could hardly eat. He spent most of his time shut up alone in his hut, not even wanting to see his friends. During this time, he did no further evangelism and even quit preaching in the church. With a thoroughly broken heart, he cried out to God, "Father, would you at least allow me to return to Britain to answer these false charges? If not, take my life now. I don't want to live any longer." But God was resolute. He wouldn't allow Patrick to leave Ireland. However, God did give Patrick the strength to stand again and resume his work.

"This will all be straightened out in eternity," Lomman comforted Patrick. "The important thing is that God knows the truth. And so do the people of Ireland."

"Besides," Secundinus chimed in, "Jesus said that a prophet is without honor in his own country. So this is nothing new."

One Sunday, Patrick preached to the congregation about the cross of Christ. He described how the enemies of Jesus had falsely accused Him of many things. They said that He blasphemed God. They alleged that He was trying to set up an earthly government in opposition to Caesar. "Sadly," Patrick pointed out, "most of the people of Jesus' day believed those false accusations. Now, God has privileged me to experience the entirety of the Christ life." Patrick then went on to explain the false accusations being made against him, how they nearly defeated him, and how God had enabled him to stand again.

"Since you can't leave Ireland to answer the charges in person, why not prepare a written rebuttal?" Secundinus suggested that afternoon.

"That's a wonderful idea, Secundinus!" Patrick replied. "Why didn't I think of it before? I guess I was feeling too sorry for myself."

So during the next week, Patrick wrote out a brief defense. He began, "I am Patrick, a sinner, most unlearned, the least of all the faithful, and utterly despised by many."[1] He then went on to describe his kidnapping as a teenager, how he was delivered by God's hands, and how God called him back to Ireland.

"I was once rustic, exiled, unlearned, and someone who did not know how to provide for the future," Patrick continued. "But this at least I know for certain: that before I was humiliated I was like a stone lying in the deep mud. And He who is mighty came and in His mercy lifted me up. He raised me up and placed me on the top of the wall. And therefore I ought to cry out aloud and so also render something to the Lord for His great benefits here and in eternity."[2] He went on to describe the suffering and dangers he was experiencing in Ireland.

Next, he addressed the false charges being made against him. "Produce even one person who has paid me for a baptism or ordination, and I will gladly return his money,"[3] he challenged his

---

[1] Patrick *Confessio §1*.

[2] Ibid. §12.

[3] Ibid. §50.

accusers. In rebuttal, he explained to his British brethren that instead of charging fees for baptism, he was having to pay tribute to various kings in order to travel through their territory. He had exhausted his entire inheritance in doing this. Finally, he wrote:

I call on God as my witness upon my soul that I am not lying. I would not write to you out of selfishness or to seek flattery. Nor am I hoping for honor from any of you. Sufficient is the honor that is not yet seen. Yet I see that even here and now, I have been exalted beyond measure by the Lord, and I was not worthy that He should grant me this. For I know most certainly that poverty and failure suit me better than wealth and delight. Therefore, may it never happen that my God would allow me to be separated from His people whom He has won in this most remote land. And if ever I have done any good for my God whom I love, I beg him to allow me to shed my blood with these exiles and captives for His name—even though I should be denied a grave, or my body be horribly torn to pieces by wild beasts.[1]

When he was finished, Patrick showed his *Testimony* to Secundinus. "It's at a time like this," Patrick confessed, "that I really regret having missed my education. I can't even write a coherent defense. And I know they'll laugh at my awkward Latin."

"Yes, but at the same time, they'll also know that it comes from your heart," Secundinus said, as he perused the *Testimony*.

The next day, Patrick sent his written *Testimony* by courier to Britain. But no one paid any attention to it. So Patrick simply had to turn the other cheek and go on with his work.[2]

---

[1]Ibid. §54-59, condensed.

[2]*Epistolo* §1, 2, 12-20; *Confessio* §50-59.

Twenty-One

From Death to Life

Patrick continued to preach the Gospel without compromise for another thirteen years. Eventually, his name was practically forgotten in Britain, although it had become a household word in Ireland. By the end of his life, he had baptized thousands and thousands of new converts and planted numerous churches throughout Ireland. Few missionaries have been as effective. Patrick rejoiced to see his native converts rise to become deacons, presbyters, and bishops themselves. Through the grace of God, Patrick outlived most of the other missionaries who labored with him, including Secundinus and Auxilius.

After a particularly exhausting evangelism tour, Patrick realized that his tired body could go no further. Returning to his hut of mud and sticks in Armagh, he spent his last days praying for the church in Ireland. Lomman–who was still living, though in poor health–tenderly looked after his every need. Finally, one day, Patrick called his close companions to his bedside.

"What day is it?" he asked. "The birds are singing so sweetly, spring must be here."

"Yes, it's March 17," Lomman answered. "Spring is just around the corner."

Patrick smiled and then counseled the men in a weak, husky voice, "Over the past thirty years, I have preached to kings and servants alike and have baptized thousands of people. Yet, if I could pass on only one lesson to you men, it would be this: I've accomplished none of these things in my own strength. No, it's all been through the grace of God. You must never ascribe these things to my own abilities or to some greatness of my own." Patrick began coughing fitfully and had to stop talking for awhile.

Finally, catching his breath, he continued, "As you men well know, we've been through a lot of trials together. I can't even recount how many times God has delivered us from injury and death. For many years now, I've realized that God was watching over me before I ever knew Him. He protected me and consoled me as a father would his son, having pity on my youth and ignorance. And so I give thanks unceasingly to Him. I particularly do so when I think about the many times that he forgave my folly and negligence. There were so many times that He had every right to be violently angry with me, yet He had mercy on me instead. I am greatly God's debtor."

"We all are," Lomman interjected.

"Yes, so remember to always exalt and magnify God's name wherever you are and regardless of what circumstances you're in. Not only when things are going well, but in affliction, too. Whatever befalls you, whether it's good or bad, accept it equally and always give thanks to God. There is still much work to be done in Ireland. So fish well and diligently. Spread out your nets so that a vast multitude and throng might be caught for God. My only wish is that you would make greater and better efforts than I did. This will be my joy, for 'a wise son makes a father glad.'"[1]

Patrick was too weak to continue any further. So he closed his eyes and slept for awhile. The other men retreated to the table at the other end of Patrick's hut. They quietly prayed and reminisced on their times with Patrick.

Suddenly, Patrick began coughing, so the men hurried to his side. Lomman quickly lifted a cup of water to his lips. When he finally stopped coughing, he lay silently in his bed, staring at his beloved companions for awhile and smiling. "I've prayed for years," Patrick said hoarsely, "that God would let me die in

---

[1] Prov. 10:1.

Ireland. And he has." Patrick closed his eyes again momentarily and smiled serenely.

Then, grasping Lomman's arm, Patrick continued, "But it's important that the Christians in Ireland keep their focus on Christ, not on me. I neither deserve nor wish for honor from any of you. Sufficient is the honor that is not yet seen, but in which my heart has confidence. I've already been exalted beyond measure by the Lord, and I wasn't worthy that He should grant me even this. God is no respecter of persons, and He chose me for this service only so I could be one of the least of His ministers. For that reason, I don't want people making pilgrimages to visit my tomb after I've died. It's important that no one give any devotion to me that should go to Christ. Accordingly, I want you all to affirm that you will bury me secretly and tell no one where I'm buried."

The men hesitated, but then gave their assurance. In a feeble voice, Patrick quietly sang some of the Psalms with the men. Finally, he asked them to come closer. He lay his quivering, gaunt hands on them, and with the last bit of his energy, he blessed them. When he finished blessing them, he joyfully welcomed death. Or, rather, he passed from death to life.[1]

---

[1] *Confessio* §34-38, 40,46,47, 54-57, 62.

Epilogue

Patrick's men were true to their word. To this day, no one knows where Patrick is buried. Yet the Irish have never forgotten him. More than fifteen hundred years after his death, he is still *the* national hero of Ireland.

However, the rest of the world had already forgotten Patrick before he died. In fact, outside of Ireland, few people had even heard of him. Those who had heard of him probably heard mainly negative things. If someone had told them that someday Patrick would be the most famous person of their age, they would have laughed derisively. No doubt, Patrick would have laughed at the thought, too. However, his name has endured, while those of his critics have disappeared.

But what about the conflict between Patrick and Coroticus? Who was right? Who did more for his country? As surprising as it may seem, Patrick helped the British far more than did Coroticus.

That's because Coroticus' savage attack on Ireland didn't stop the pagan Irish raiders from attacking Britain again. But Patrick's work did! Within a few decades after his death, the vast majority of the Irish had become Christians. And once the Irish embraced Christ, they no longer assaulted the British coast. In the end, the man of faith protected his country better than the man of war!

But there's more to the story. Patrick's converts and their descendants actively befriended the British people. They gave considerable help to the struggling British church and allowed many of the British to settle in Ireland, as a safe haven from the Saxons. Instead of sending out boatloads of warriors, Ireland began sending out boatloads of missionaries! These missionaries were rugged men of prayer who closely followed the example of Patrick. One such missionary, Columba, sailed to Scotland, bringing the gospel to the pagan Picts there. After his death, another Irish Christian, Aidan, came to northern England and converted thousands of the pagan Saxons. Inspired by the example of the Irish church, the native British church finally found a way to love their enemies, the Saxons, and to bring them to Christ. So Patrick's mission to the Irish not only forever changed Ireland, it was the seminal event that eventually brought Christianity to Scotland and England.

Lessons from Patrick's Life

Perhaps the most important thing we can learn from Patrick's life is that there is incredible power in prayer. But if we want to fully experience this power, we should not think we can get by with merely praying once or twice for something. No, we've got to pound on the doors of heaven night and day, never letting up—just like Patrick did. Thousands of other Christians were taken captive around the same time as he. No doubt, nearly all of them prayed to God for deliverance. Yet, very few of them received the same answer that he did. That's because they neither prayed long enough, nor often enough. Perhaps some of them prayed diligently for the first six months or so of their captivity. But then, when their prayers weren't answered, they began slacking off. Suppose someone had interviewed them ten years after they had been captured and asked them about the power of prayer. They would have probably said that prayer doesn't work.

However, perhaps the reason they didn't receive an answer to their prayers is because they didn't pray like Patrick. They didn't keep pounding on the doors of heaven. That's a lesson we Christians must never forget. What would have happened if Patrick had only prayed once or twice a day, instead of a hundred times or more. He would have probably spent his entire life as a slave in Ireland. What if he had prayed for only six *months,* instead of six *years*? The only sheep he would have shepherded would have been Milchu's. What if he had given up on prayer after five and a half years? He may have spent the rest of his life as a bitter man, having lost all confidence in the power of prayer.

So if we want to experience God's power, we must pray powerfully. If we want God to do great things through us–as He did in Patrick, we must be great men and women of prayer. God might accomplish through us the same things He did in Patrick, if only we would pray like him. Very few of us ever taste the full power of God because we make too little time—or have too little faith—to keep knocking on the doors of heaven. Most of us think that if we spend one whole day in prayer and fasting, we've accomplished some Herculean task! We expect God to be so impressed that He will immediately grant our petitions. But it doesn't usually work that way. Praise God that in His mercy, He does frequently answer our prayers favorably, even when we don't persist in prayer. But most Christians never encounter God in His fullness, the way Patrick did, because we don't pray like Patrick.

Another important lesson that Patrick has left us is the need to wait on God. At first glance, it may seem that Patrick would have accomplished more if he had not waited for twenty-five years on the church in Britain to send him. However, in reality, God needed those twenty-five years to finish the work He had begun in him. In fact, God's *normal* course of action is to require His servants to learn to wait on Him.

When he chose Moses, He didn't immediately use him to deliver the children of Israel. No, he made Moses spend forty years in the wilderness. During those forty years, Moses was a seemingly forgotten shepherd. From a human perspective, those years might seem like forty wasted years. But in God's perspective, those years were absolutely essential. God was patiently molding and mellowing this hot-headed firebrand named Moses. When God was finished, Moses was the meekest man on earth. God could now speak to him face to face. Quite often God chooses passionate zealots as his instruments. In some ways, Patrick was such a person. But before God can use zealots, He has to first re-mold them. He doesn't quench their fire, but He does teach them to wait on Him.

Paul was such a man, too. He began as a hot-headed firebrand who fought against Christianity. After his encounter with Jesus on the road to Damascus, he became a hot-headed firebrand fighting *for* Christianity. Yet, before God could use Paul to plant churches and build up the body of Christ, He required him to spend ten or eleven quiet years in places like Syria and the Arabian wilderness. To human eyes, Paul seemed to have dropped out of sight. But he was in the center of God's focus, because God was molding and mellowing Paul. When God was finished with His schooling, he let Paul loose. And the church hasn't been the same ever since!

It's so easy to forget that God's timetable is different from ours. We usually want things *now*! But God operates on a time scale in which a thousand years is only a day. In our eyes, it seems that Patrick had to wait six long years in Ireland before God delivered him from slavery. However, in God's timetable, he waited less than nine minutes. In our eyes, Patrick had to wait twenty-five years before being able to return to Ireland. However, in God's timetable, he waited only about forty minutes.

What would have happened if Patrick had run ahead of God and gone to Ireland as an independent maverick? No doubt he would still have had a measure of success. God doesn't necessarily destroy our work because we run ahead of Him. On the other hand, He rarely gives it His full blessing, either. If Patrick had run ahead of God, no doubt many of the Irish still would have come to Christ. Maybe a hundred or more. Perhaps, even as many as a thousand. But it's unlikely that thousands would have received the Gospel, as they did. In other words, if Patrick had begun his work in Ireland *sooner*, he would have accomplished *less*. That's because his human contribution to the work was significantly less than God's contribution—just as he so often acknowledged. By waiting on God, he received the full blessing of God.

Just like the church in Patrick's day, today's church faces many crises. My prayer is that God will raise up a Patrick for our day. But if so, who will he be? A famous Christian author or televangelist? Someone heading up a well-known ministry? A familiar speaker who talks at various churches and frequently appears on Christian talk shows? Not likely.

If there's a potential Patrick around today, I doubt any of us have ever heard of him. That's because he's off alone tending sheep somewhere—or on his knees in his closet—praying to God.

Appendix One

Was Patrick Roman Catholic?

The average Christian today would no doubt tell a questioner that Patrick was Roman Catholic. However, as we have seen, he wasn't. He belonged to the independent, autonomous Celtic or British church. To be sure, the British church of his day had contacts with the Pope, but it was not under the Pope's authority.[1] It was—and had always been—a self-governing church.[2]

More than that, the Celtic church of Patrick's day bore only faint resemblance to medieval and modern Roman Catholicism. It knew nothing of purgatory, indulgences, the infallibility of the pope, transubstantiation, and a whole host of other Roman Catholic dogmas. Celtic Christians of Patrick's day didn't use holy water, pray with a rosary, or say masses to deliver the dead from purgatory. Patrick never taught his converts to pray to saints. In fact, in his writings, Patrick uses the word *saint* in its original sense to apply to all godly Christians. For example, he writes in his *Testimony*, "How I would have loved to go to my country and my parents, and also to Gaul in order to visit the brethren and to

---

[1] In his writings, Patrick makes no references whatsoever to Rome or to the Pope. It was medieval biographers with Roman Catholic leanings who invented stories about Patrick being sent to Ireland by the Pope. Today, even Roman Catholic scholars acknowledge that Patrick was not Roman Catholic and that the Pope had not commissioned him.

[2] Christianity had not come to Britain from Rome. In fact, it very likely came to Britain from the East. That's why the Celtic or British church followed different customs than Rome.

see the faces of the saints of my Lord!"[1]

Furthermore, in his writings, Patrick makes no references to relics (bones of apostles and saints). He didn't perform cures through relics, nor did he encourage his converts to venerate relics. In fact, there is no evidence that he ever brought any relics of any kind with him to Ireland. Likewise, Patrick didn't use any statues or icons in his churches. That's why the oldest surviving Christian cemeteries, churches, and monastic cells in Ireland contain no statues, painted icons, or carvings of any kind—other than simple crosses.

It is common knowledge that Roman Catholic priests must be celibate. However, Patrick knew nothing of such mandatory celibacy. After all, his own grandfather was a married priest! More precisely, I should say he was a married presbyter. It was after Patrick's time that British Christians used "priest" as a synonym for "presbyter." Patrick himself never used the word "priest" in his writings. Rather, he refers to his grandfather as a *presbyterus*[2]—a Latin transliteration of the Greek word *presbyteros*. It's also noteworthy that he confessed his serious childhood sin to a fellow *layman* (his traitorous friend), not to a priest.

Current statues and pictures of Patrick have helped to perpetuate the myth that he was Roman Catholic. That's because they invariably portray him as traveling throughout Ireland wearing a bishop's robe and mitre.[3] However, the sculptors and illustrators who produce these items obviously have not done their homework. In Patrick's day, no bishops roamed about in special clerical garb. That didn't come along until the Middle Ages. Furthermore, bishops in the West did not begin wearing mitres until the eleventh century—about six hundred years after Patrick was dead! Patrick

---

[1] *Confessio* §43.

[2] Ibid. §1.

[3] A mitre is the tall pointed hat worn by Roman Catholic and Anglican bishops.

was not a Roman Catholic bishop. In fact, he didn't even *look* like one.

Perhaps the most striking difference between Patrick's Christianity and Roman Catholicism concerns Mary. Mariology and Mariolatry have dominated Roman Catholicism for the last fourteen hundred years. In contrast, Patrick never refers to Mary at all in his writings. Throughout all of his hardships and perils, he never once cried out to Mary. Rather, he called out either to the Father or to Jesus. Similarly, Patrick knew nothing of the various Roman Catholic dogmas about Mary—such as the immaculate conception, her ascension to heaven, and her reigning as queen of heaven.

The Last of the Primitive Christians

If Patrick wasn't Roman Catholic, what was he? As I've mentioned, he was a member of the autonomous Celtic or British Church. But more than that, Patrick can perhaps best be described simply as a primitive or early Christian. He bore most of the distinguishing characteristics of primitive Christianity.

The essence of primitive Christianity was not theology, but an obedient love relationship with Christ. This was also the core of Patrick's Christianity. He was no theologian, nor were any of his disciples. Patrick instilled in his disciples a love of Christ, not a love of theology. In fact, the Irish church has never produced any great theologians—yet it has raised up some of the finest mission-aries in the world.

Another characteristic of the early Christians is that they strongly believed in separation of church and state. They didn't try to mix the things of this world with the things of the kingdom of God. Similarly, Patrick did not establish a state church in Ireland, nor did he try to blend Christianity with the affairs of this world. The early Christians obeyed Caesar, so long as his laws didn't conflict with God's commandments. But when his laws violated those of God, the early Christians obeyed God rather than man. Likewise, Patrick showed deference to secular rulers, so long as their demands didn't conflict with God's. For example, he paid them tribute when they demanded it. However, he showed no partiality to them when it came to spiritual matters. He didn't hesitate to excommunicate them, and he would not accept gifts from unbaptized or excommunicated kings.

Another distinction of the primitive Christians is that they never used the sword or compulsion from earthly kings to spread the Gospel. They offered no earthly enticements or social advantages to their converts. Yet the early church grew rapidly, converting a large percentage of the Roman Empire. Like the primitive Christians before him, Patrick didn't use the sword or secular power to convert his hearers. The only social advantage he could offer a convert was access to reading and writing. In fact, much of what he taught went contrary to Irish culture. Patrick depended on the power of the Holy Spirit to change lives, not on the power of this world. His hearers became Christians because of their personal faith in Jesus Christ. The Christianity that Patrick planted in Ireland was a vibrant Christianity that emphasized prayer, fasting, holy living, and evangelism.

How Ireland Became Roman Catholic

If Patrick's converts were not Roman Catholic, why is Ireland so staunchly Roman Catholic today? The answer is that Roman Catholicism came to Ireland by the sword. The popes had always resented the independent church in Ireland, but they were unable to bring it under Roman domination. In fact, the popes were also displeased with the Anglo-Saxon church in England. Even though the English Church eventually became Roman Catholic, it resisted many of Rome's practices, such as forced celibacy. For that reason, the Pope had encouraged the invasion of England in 1066 by William the Conqueror. The Pope wanted William to bring the

English Church in line with the rest of Roman Catholicism.

William and his heavily armed Norman knights defeated Harold the Saxon at the Battle of Hastings, and William was crowned King of England. As king, William worked swiftly to overhaul Anglo-Saxon laws and government and to bring the English church into conformity with Rome. Once William and his successors had accomplished this, the Pope turned his attention to Ireland. In 1169, Pope Adrian issued a papal bull granting the entire nation of Ireland to Henry II, the Norman king of England.[1] At the Pope's behest, several of Henry's warlords invaded Ireland. These "Christian" invaders slaughtered men, women, and children and butchered presbyters and monks. They tore down many of the huts of the Irish monks and built Roman Catholic monasteries in their places. The independent church of Ireland was snuffed out.

Why the Irish Rejected the Reformation

Given the fact that Roman Catholicism had been forced on the Irish, a person might logically expect the Irish to have been among the first people to embrace the Reformation. And perhaps they would have—if it had not been for the irony of several subsequent historical events. After the Norman warlords completed their conquest of Ireland in the twelfth century, they intermarried with the Irish and soon adopted the Irish language and customs. As a result, their loyalty to England weakened, and Ireland practically became independent once again. So in the sixteenth century, Henry VIII of England found it necessary to use strong-arm tactics to bring Ireland back under English rule. Not surprisingly, his brutal tactics alienated the Irish people. So when Henry broke from Rome, the Irish were not about to follow his lead. The Irish decided to remain Roman Catholic, rather than to follow anything initiated by Henry VIII.

---

[1]Henry II was a direct descendant of William the Conqueror.

When the Irish didn't voluntarily accept Henry's ecclesiastical reforms, he tried to force his changes upon the Irish. But his harsh tactics only made the Irish even more devoted to Rome. Later, Queen Elizabeth I went so far as to outlaw Roman Catholic services in Ireland and to execute a number of Irish Roman Catholic bishops and priests.

In response, the Irish rebelled numerous times against English rule and English Protestantism. However, up until the twentieth century, the English armies swiftly and decisively put down all of the Irish revolts. Each time, the English government imposed new punishments on Ireland. In fact, the English rulers eventually took most of the land in Ireland away from the Roman Catholic Irish and gave it to English Protestant settlers.

As a result of these things, the cause of Irish liberty and Roman Catholicism became intertwined and have remained so to this day. That's why Ireland is still staunchly Roman Catholic. And that is why there is still so much tension in Northern Ireland between the Irish Roman Catholics and the British Protestants.

Appendix Two

Notes

Chapter Seven

Patrick doesn't name the land to which the Irish sailors took him. The traditional view is that it was Gaul, which I believe is the most plausible position. Some modern scholars speculate that the sailors took him to Britain. However, it seems virtually impossible that Patrick and the sailors could have wandered for twenty-eight days in Britain without encountering any inhabitants.

In the middle of his narrative about his escape from Ireland and his trials with the Irish sailors, Patrick states: "And once again, after many years, I was taken captive. On the first night I stayed with them, I heard a divine message saying to me, 'You will be with them for two months.' And so it happened that on the sixtieth night thereafter the Lord delivered me out of their hands"[1] I interpret this second captivity of sixty days to be referring to Patrick's time of servitude with the Irish sailors. However, other historians interpret it to mean that Patrick was taken captive still another time.

Chapter Twelve

Patrick doesn't tell us what country he was in when the presbyters considered ordaining him as a bishop. Armorica (Brittany) is only one possibility.

Concerning his episcopacy, Patrick states: "I was attacked by a number of my seniors, who brought up my sins against my arduous episcopate. ...As cause for proceeding against me, they brought

---

[1]*Confessio* §21

174

up—after thirty years!—a confession I had made before I was a deacon. In the anxiety of my troubled mind I confided to my dearest friend what I had done in my boyhood. ...On that day, then, I was rejected by those referred to."[1] I interpret this passage to refer to the time when Patrick's seniors first considered ordaining him as a bishop. However, some historians believe this passage is referring to one of the attacks on Patrick after he had already been ordained as a bishop.

Chapter Fourteen

In his writings, Patrick does not relate how he presented the gospel to his first hearers. Tradition tells us that the first king to whom he presented the gospel was Laoghaire. For my narration of Patrick's first presentation of the gospel, I have primarily used statements and thoughts from his *Testimony*.

Chapter Fifteen

We don't know for certain that Patrick used "seeds of truth" in Irish culture to help present the gospel. However, this was the typical method of witnessing used by early Christian evangelists, as illustrated by the works of such early Christians as Justin Martyr, Athenagoras, and Tertullian.

Chapter Twenty-One

Patrick's farewell exhortation has been taken almost verbatim from his *Testimony*. Needless to say, Patrick penned his *Testimony* prior to his death, so we don't know for certain that he repeated this counsel on his deathbed.

Who's Who in Patrick's Life

Patrick supplies very few names of his contemporaries in his

---

[1] *Confessio §26, 27, 29.*

writings. At other times, he provides a name, but gives no description of who the person is. To relate the story of Patrick's life in a manner that realistically describes the world he lived in, I've tried to bring to life the various persons who are only briefly described or hinted at in his writings.

The following summary explains which figures in my account are (1) historical persons directly described by Patrick or Bede[1], (2) figures described in ancient traditions about Patrick, or (3) true-to-life literary figures created to embody persons who are briefly mentioned or intimated in Patrick's works.

Ailbe. Irish deacon slain by Coroticus' soldiers. Name is traditional; character is literary. Embodies one of the men whom Coroticus and his soldiers slew.

Auxilius. Fellow-worker of Patrick in Ireland. Traditional.

Brannoc. British bishop who is friendly to Patrick. Literary. Embodies British clergy described by Patrick.

Bron. Irish convert. Name is traditional; character is literary. Embodies those converts whom Patrick says remained celibate.

Calpornius. Patrick's father. Historic.

Cedd. Patrick's fellow slave in Ireland. Literary. Embodies the thousands of Christians that Patrick says were enslaved in Ireland at the same time he was.

Concessa. Patrick's mother. Traditional. Patrick makes no direct mention of his mother in his works, although he does speak of his "parents." Ancient traditions give her name as Concessa.

Coirpre. King who treacherously imprisoned Patrick and his men. Person is historic; name is traditional.

---

[1]Using older written documents, Bede wrote his invaluable *Ecclesiastical History of the English People* in 731.

Coroticus. British king who raided Ireland. Historic. Described at length in Patrick's letter of excommunication. Many scholars identify him with Ceredig, the self-made British king and hero, and I have followed that interpretation in my account.

Crispus. Deacon who accompanied Patrick to Ireland. Name is literary; person is traditional.

Donabhan. Son of Milchu, Patrick's master. Literary.

Ethne. Young Irish woman. Historic. Patrick describes her as "a blessed Irish woman of noble birth, beautiful, full-grown, whom I had baptized."[1] He then describes how "a messenger of God" admonished her to remain celibate. Her name comes from tradition.

Fedelm and Fedilmid. Daughter and son of King Laoghaire. Persons and names are traditional. In his *Testimony*, Patrick specifically states that he converted "sons and daughters of the kings of the Irish."[2]

Hengest and Horsa. The two Saxon chieftains who first came to Britain. Historic.

Julius. British bishop. Literary. Embodies British clergy whom Patrick describes.

Laoghaire. King to whom Patrick first preached the gospel. Traditional.

Lomman. Presbyter who accompanied Patrick to Ireland and who tried to secure the release of the Irish Christians whom Coroticus had kidnapped. Person is historic; name is from tradition. Patrick describes him as "a holy presbyter whom I had taught from childhood."[3]

---

[1] *Confessio* §42.

[2] Ibid. §41.

[3] *Epistolo* §3.

Mac Fechnach. Excommunicated king who tried to make a gift to Patrick. Person is literary; name is from tradition. Embodies those of whom Patrick wrote, "Many gifts were offered to me in sorrow and tears, and I offended the donors, much against the wishes of some of my seniors."[1]

Marcella. Patrick's former nurse who was kidnapped with him. Literary. Embodies the "servants and maids of my father's house"[2] who Patrick says were taken captive with him.

Marcus. Patrick's friend who betrayed him. Person is historic; name is literary. Patrick describes his false friend in his *Testimony* and relates how this friend betrayed him. However, he mercifully does not reveal his false friend's name.

Milchu. Patrick's master when he was a slave in Ireland. Person is historic; name is traditional.

Petronius. British presbyter. Literary. Embodies the British presbyters about whom Patrick writes.

Potitus. Patrick's grandfather. Historic.

Quintus. Presbyter who opposed Patrick. Literary. Embodies the presbyters that Patrick refers to when he writes, "I was attacked by a number of my seniors who came forth and brought up my sins against my laborious episcopate."[3] Also embodies the "seniors" who rebuked Patrick for not accepting gifts from sinners and the unbaptized.

Secundinus. Patrick's fellow-worker in Ireland. Traditional.

Teilo. The barber in Bannavem Taburniae. Literary.

---

[1] *Confessio* §37.

[2] *Epistolo* §10.

[3] *Confessio* §26.

Victoricus. Historic and literary. Patrick relates that in his dream Victoricus came from Ireland with letters from the Irish. The fact that Patrick gives no further description of him indicates that he was a well-known Christian in Patrick's community.

Vortigern. Historic. Identified by Bede as the leader who convinced his fellow Britons to invite the Saxons to settle in Britain.

Bibliography

Primary and Ancient Sources

Bede. *Ecclesiastical History of the English People*. Translated by Leo Sherley-Price. New York: Viking Penguin, Inc. 1990.

Bede, et al. *The Age of Bede*. Translated by J. F. Webb and D. H. Farmer. New York: Viking Penguin, Inc. 1983.

Marcellinus, Ammianus. *The Later Roman Empire*. Translated by Walter Hamilton. New York: Viking Penguin, Inc. 1986.

Patrick. *The Works of St. Patrick*. Translated by Ludwig Bieler. New York: Newman Press. 1953.

Roberts, Alexander and Donaldson, James, eds. *The AnteNicene Fathers*. 10 vols. Peabody: Hendrickson Publishers, Inc. 1995.

Schaff, Philip and Wace, Henry. eds. *The Nicene and Post-Nicene Fathers, Second Series*. 14 vols. Peabody: Hendrickson Publishers, Inc. 1995.

Tacitus. *The Agricola and the Germania*. Translated by H. Mattingly. New York: Viking Penguin, Inc. 1948.

Secondary Sources

Blair, Peter Hunter. *Roman Britain and Early England*. New York: W. W. Norton & Company. 1963.

Bury, J. B. *The Life of St. Patrick*. New York: The Macmillan Company. 1905.

Dumville, David. *Saint Patrick, A.D. 493-1993*. New York: The Boydell Press. 1993.

Fry, Peter and Fiona. *A History of Ireland*. New York: Routledge. 1988.

Herm, Gerhard. *The Celts: The People Who Came out of the Darkness*. New York: St. Martin's Press. 1976.

Marnell, William. *Light from the West*. New York: The Seabury Press. 1978.

Norton-Taylor, Duncan. *The Celts*. New York: Time-Life Books, Inc. 1974.

Ottaway, Patrick and Michael Cyprien. *A Traveller's Guide to Roman Britain*. London: Routledge & Kegan Paul.1987.

Quennell, Marjorie & C. H. B. *Everyday Life in Roman Britain*. New York: G. P. Putnam's Son. 1924.

Ross, Anne and Robins, Don. *The Life and Death of a Druid Prince*. New York: Summit Books. 1989.

Schaff, Philip. *History of the Christian Church*. 8 vols. Grand Rapids: Wm. B. Eerdmans Publishing Company, 1910.

Scullard, H. H. *Roman Britain*. London: Thames and Hudson Ltd. 1979.

Thompson, E. A. *Who Was Saint Patrick?* New York: St. Martin's Press. 1985.

Toulson, Shirley. *The Celtic Year*. Rockport: Element, Inc. 1993.

Other works by the same author:

The Kingdom That Turned The World Upside Down

If someone were to ask you what was the theme of Jesus' preaching, what would be your answer? Man's need for salvation? God's love for mankind? The new birth? To be sure, Jesus spoke about all of those things. And they're all essential truths. But none of them were the *theme* of His teaching. The theme of Jesus' message was the *kingdom of God.*

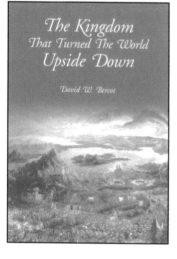

The irony is that the message of the kingdom is almost totally missing from the gospel that's preached today. As a result, a lot of Christians don't even know what the kingdom of God is.

In *The Kingdom That Turned the World Upside Down,* David Bercot takes the reader back to Jesus' teachings of the kingdom — teachings that have too often been forgotten. Bercot describes the radically new laws of the kingdom and its upside-down values. This book will challenge you to the core in your Christian walk! **$9.95**

To order your copy, or to obtain a free catalog of all of our publications, please contact us: **www.scrollpublishing.com**

(717) 349-7033 ● P. O. Box 122 ● Amberson, PA 17210

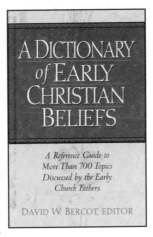